The
PHILOSOPHY
of
INSPIRATION

The
PHILOSOPHY
of
INSPIRATION

Mirgandra Agarwal

NEW DAWN PRESS, INC.
UK • USA • INDIA

NEW DAWN PRESS GROUP

Published by New Dawn Press Group
New Dawn Press, Inc., 244 South Randall Rd # 90, Elgin, IL 60123
e-mail: sales@newdawnpress.com

New Dawn Press, 2 Tintern Close, Slough, Berkshire, SL1-2TB, UK
e-mail: ndpuk@newdawnpress.com

New Dawn Press (An Imprint of Sterling Publishers (P) Ltd.)
A-59, Okhla Industrial Area, Phase-II, New Delhi-110020
e-mail: info@sterlingpublishers.com
www.sterlingpublishers.com

The Philosophy of Inspiration
©2005, Mirgandra Agarwal
ISBN 1 84557 280 7

All rights are reserved. No part of this publication may be reproduced, stored in a retrieval system or transmitted, in any form or by any means, mechanical, photocopying, recording or otherwise, without prior written permission of the publisher.

PRINTED IN INDIA

Dedicated to
Vedic past living in present
and
Future hope living in younger generation
including
my twelve-year-old grandson Ajay Agarwal

Preface

In the seventies of the last century believers began to use violence, murder and destruction in the name of religion. Since then terror has become the technique and policy of religions to gain political ends, which cannot be achieved by peaceful means. It has encouraged me to read and study great religions to find the thread of this carnage and mayhem.

I began to study and understand Aryan religion. The following chapters are the result of my study and understanding. This book is written for an ordinary and simple soul who is enthusiastic, motivated, and has a burning desire to be worthy of him and others. For a dedicated and sincere reader this book could supply ingredients of conceiving a vision that may give birth to inspiration in him. Learning music or reading a book is not enough, one has to be inspired to become a musician or a creative writer.

It is my observation that Vedic literature contains three religions; it developed in stages in the interval of about three to five thousand years before the birth of Christ – from *Rig Veda* to the great epics, the *Mahabharata* and the *Ramayana*. One religion is of four Vedas – to worship natural objects like sun, moon, rivers, mountains trees, animals, etc. as *deva*s through prayers, rituals and sacrifices. Prayers are sung in their honour and power; sacrifices are made to force them to comply with the wishes of devotees. These compiled and conceived hymns of prayers are originals, found in the history of civilisation.

Life cannot be conceived without the natural phenomenon of sun, moon, fire, water, mountains, etc. as these help to sustain life on earth. Everyone can sing the hymns and *mantras* for the help they provide to us. The singing of hymns is not exclusive to Aryans or Hindus; anyone can share the value and importance of the natural phenomenon by singing with devotion. In a democratic country like India, Muslims, Christians and Hindus can pay their debt to these natural objects.

The second religion of the Vedic literature is the religion of the Upanishad*s*. With the passage of thousands of years sages came to the conclusion that nature is changeable and hence cannot be considered as God, for God is changeless, and around him everything revolves. The same is equally true with one's state of mind. Pleasure is followed by pain, happiness by sorrow, fear by courage. But the question that baffled sages was, "Is change itself the ultimate reality, or is any changeless essence the basis of all change?"

A clue was ultimately found to the mystery of knowledge, and sages discovered that by knowing, for example, the nature of clay one knows the nature of everything made of clay. The search of this One led to the nature of man himself. Therefore, the study of man opened a new chapter in the discovery of God in man.

One should search God within and not outside. It has shifted the approach of the Vedic sages from nature to man himself. The worship of the outer phenomena of the Vedas had been transferred to the study and knowledge of the inner self. It is the knowledge of the unborn and the unseen prescribed in the Upanishad*s* or the Vedanta. The new gods of the Upanishad*s* arrived in the form of Brahman or Atman.

The third religion of Vedic literature is the religion of Sutras and Puranas that led the worship of forms, images or idols like Shiva, Vishnu, Brahma, Ganesh, Lakshmi, etc. For the first time in the Vedic age worship of these visible gods in the forms of images was practised in temples. The chief object of worshipping an image of God was to understand the invisible with the medium of visible images. Idol worship was evolved for children, women, traders, agriculturists, and the lesser members of the society, as they were not competent enough to comprehend the invisible Brahman of the Upanishads. As an analogy, one can comprehend the sound of music only by observing the musical instruments.

If we go further in the realm of Vedic literature, the sources of two other religions can be traced in it—Buddhism and Jainism. The superstructure of these religions are based on Vedic literature just as the New Testament of Christianity is based on the Old Testament of Judaism; just as the religion of the shrine of Ka'bah originated from the temple of Abraham, where believers of other religions of Arab population used to go for worship.

The great scholars of Germany from Goethe to Herman Hess nurtured the glory of Vedic literature in the last three hundred years with great zeal and enthusiasm. India owes a great deal to Germany who has presented the Vedic spirit to Europe and rest of the world with sincerity and honesty. It can safely be said that Germany is the second home of Vedic literature. Von Schroeder says, 'The Indians are romanticists of the ancient, and the Germans are the romanticists of the modern." G Brandes remarks, "The tendency towards contemplation and abstract speculation is common between Indians and Germans." Indian and German cultures are similar in many other ways. It is only German poets, who have sung sorrow,

> Sweet is sleep
> But death is better,
> Best of all is not to be born.

It is the voice of the Upanishads and Buddha, sung by a German poet. Again, sentimentality and feelings are the common property of Germans and Indians. Indians love description of nature expressed in the Vedas and by poet Kalidasa, so too do the Germans. There is another similarity—the Indians are the scholars of the past and the Germans are the scholars of the present. The Germans are undisputed leaders in all fields of philology and linguistic science based on the scientific system on Indian classification of linguistic phenomena. Even before the birth of Christ, grammar was the passion of India, where it was studied with great enthusiasm –a study in which Indians led all other nations in the ancient world. Panini, the great grammarian of the ancient era, recognised that before him 64 generations had contributed more in ancient India.

There are not very many English scholars or writers who have done good quality work on Vedic literature like the Germans. Whatever work has been done by English authors, was carried out due to the administrative needs of the colonial rulers to govern India. The first was Sir William Jones who established the Asiatic Society in 1784, and translated two plays of poet Kalidasa and the code of law book of Manu. The other English name of repute is Colebooke who, at the beginning of the nineteenth century, handled the Vedic literature on scientific lines and published many translations and textbooks. The next is A. B. Keith who also did good quality work on Vedic literature. Sir Edwin Arnold drew his inspirations from Sanskrit literature for all his works including *Light of Asia*. Another Englishman, indirectly associated, is Alexander Hamilton who taught Sanskrit to a German, named Fredrick Schlegel, in Paris in 1802 for six years. Later, Schlegel published a book on *The Language and Wisdom of Indians* in 1808. It produced a revolution and aroused great interest in Vedic literature in Germany.

Britain devoted and invested most of her talents in the development of diplomatic skills. It has not helped mankind in the way Germans have contributed to the welfare of mankind.

Preface

All the empires, as history reveals, went to ruins and left their imprints of history. The great contribution to the world by India, Greece and Germany will always be etched in the annals of history. Additions to population, increase in territories – these are not growth in the spirit but rather a warning of misery and calamity in the future.

Non-Muslim or European scholars have not done much serious work on Islam. Whatever work has been carried out has been done mostly by Muslim scholars or religious leaders. The aim of non-Muslim scholars is to provide the basic facts and general opinion about the religion and not to enlighten the reader with the finer points of Islam. It came to my notice during the reading of Islamic literature that Ummah was established in the neighbourhood in AD 620 as a secular club or Commonwealth of Jews, Christians and Arabs to collect taxes from those who went on a pilgrimage via Medinah to the shrine of Ka'bah. Prophet Mohammed was its arbiter. A few years later, by AD 632 it became non-secular based on the teachings and practices of the prophet. Secondly, political and religious authority merged into one.

So far as Christianity is concerned Christians and non-Christian scholars and spiritual leaders have done enough work of the highest quality throughout the whole world almost in every language.

Buddhism is also a great religion. I would like to quote the teachings of Lord Buddha in the following words. Once Buddha declared in one of his sermons to his disciples, "Do not believe what you have heard; do not believe in doctrines because they have been handed down to you of generations; do not believe in anything because it is followed by many and majority; do not believe some old monk or preacher who makes a statement; do not believe in the truth to which you have become attached by habit; do not believe merely on authority of your teacher and elders; have deliberations and analyse; and when the result agrees with reason and is conducive to the good of one and all, accept it and live unto it."

Today, all religions are trying to make man evolve into a 'better man' on the basis of prescribed doctrines and dogmas from authoritative structures, and end up making him a devil or monster. They should try making God out of man. For the evolution of a better man religions were instituted, each with an authority. This authority is the root of all evil. The pronouncements and declarations of the religious authority were treated as words from God, which had to be obeyed. Those who dared to defy were treated as being blasphemous and dealt with accordingly.

Economic and political interests that fashion the action and behaviour of groups and governments of the day should to help making the societies noble. We advocate love while practise hatred. We preach peace while practise violence. We are dishonest while propagate honesty in our dealings. We play politics and diplomacy while act in self-interest. We form international organisations while encourage nationalism. We seek justice while deal in double standards. We talk of equality while use discrimination. We hide our lies and expect truth from others. Once Dr Radhakrishnan wrote that the Security Council was like a kindergarten of delinquent children who display the might of their costly toys to force others to toe the line of the rich and powerful; otherwise dire consequences will follow.

It was Gandhi who used love against brutality, non-violence against violence, self-resistance against force, practised truth against diplomacy, and lived a simple life like shining wealth. In the words of Dr Abdul Kalam, India needs a second vision to put the country in the league of developed nations, thereby creating an intellectual revolution of the ancient India which could last longer than thousands of years. In his opinion it is possible if we look at our younger generations who are the future builders and guardians, having the capacity to conceive a vision that will give birth to inspirations. Until now the younger generations in India have been ignored. Leaders believed that they had the exclusive right and authority to walk on the road of progress leaving behind the younger generation at their mercy.

Once Dr Kalam visited a secondary school and questioned a pupil in the assembly, "Who is the enemy of India?" An eighteen-year-old girl replied, "Unemployment and poverty." The whole staff, including the visitor, agreed with the answer of the girl. A few months later, Dr Kalam published a book and dedicated it to the girl. This is the way to fill the minds of our youngsters with vision and inspiration, as such acts will motivate and inspire the younger India.

Another story in the life of Dr Kalam reveals the true man in him. When friends and foes raised the question of religion, that he was not a true Muslim, for he read Hindu scriptures like the *Gita* and *Vedas*, etc. his reply to the critics was that he was divine in the sense that the same divinity resides in everyone else. Therefore there is no religion involved. It is in everybody and one has to give wings to one's divinity by hard work. One has to discover God within oneself. Religion is not a weapon to destroy property and murder thousands; rather it is a shield to protect and preserve life. Those who dare to fly will be blessed with the heights. Once you are on the path of destiny, the whole universe will conspire in your favour.

Gandhi and Dr Kalam are similar to our ancient sages. They are realists and rationalists who did not believe in the finished product of the artists; rather they preferred to supply raw material into modelling hands of the people. To produce the finished product like an artist is to limit the intelligence and wisdom of the people. They are to be judged by what they are rather than what they have achieved in life. The Vedic rishis did not leave their names behind as they were more interested in seeking truth rather than have their names glorified. On the contrary, successive generations glorified the names of the distinguished people and had them honoured and respected.

The ocean does not put any limit or restriction upon the water that you carry from it; it is the limitations of your pot that restrict how much you can carry. The sun does not control its light from one house to another but it is the walls of your house that deny the entry of sunlight into your house. Medicine cannot create health; it only helps to remove the causes of ill health. It is not the fault of the road if you have an accident; the weakness lies in your driving that causes an accident. Therefore, it is you and no one else who can expand your growth. We have conquered nature but failed to conquer ourselves. We have mastered the scientific knowledge but failed to use it for the good of mankind. We have delivered the baby but failed to bring him up adequately and properly.

What is natural is original, pure and glorious and does not need support or encouragement, whereas what is unnatural or man-made requires efforts, force, propaganda and persuasion to expand to be popular. Nature is free and independent and the unnatural is dependent and without substance of its own. Nature has evolutions and no history. God who dwells in man has no history. Nature provides trees full of fruits, which are alike yet are not identical in size, shape and colour, i.e., pale, green, big or small. When fruits become ripe they are sweet. Sweetness is invisible in fruits and cannot be known from outside. The same is true with man that God cannot be known from outside. When man becomes enriched in knowledge of the Unseen and the Unborn he finds God in him. The Upanishads have proved it beyond a shadow of doubt that man is God and one has to comprehend it.

A leaf is not a creation of the tree but a mini tree. A drop of water is not the creation of the ocean but a mini ocean. A stone is not a creation of the mountain but a mini mountain. An investigation of a drop of human blood reveals the condition of the body and not the creation of the body. The relationship of ice and water, relationship of stone and mountain is not the relationship of creation or creator but the manifestation of the unity with each other. The building of a church, mosque or temple is an abode of God and the spirit of divinity behind it. The body of a human being is like the building of a church, mosque or temple in which resides God and the spirit of divinity. To kill or harm the body by any pretext, even in war, is a crime against the spirit of divinity. By destroying the mosque or temple you destroy the spirit. God never advocates murder, slaughter and hatred. There is only one religion of man, irrespective of different cultures and creeds—to love and to realise unity with God like a drop seeks unity with the waters of the ocean. The rest is artificial and creates authority over fellow beings. The theory and practice of love is the greatest battle that man has to conquer before making his body pure and free from hatred, murder and fear.

Religion is a law of inner growth and not a duty imposed from outside. It is a sense of internal discipline. A spark is not only a spark but it has great potentials to destroy large monuments in a second, and man has the same spark or spirit with great potentials to realise God within himself.

Once a humble person went to Mecca to see the shrine of Ka'bah. After reaching the shrine he felt very tired and immediately fell asleep. He was woken up rudely by an Imam, who shouted at him, "Kafir, do you know that while sleeping you should not have your legs pointing towards the holy Ka'bah? Get up and turn around." The humble man replied, "Brother, why do you get angry for a simple thing like this? You may turn down my leg any side you think the Lord is not present." The

Imam turned his legs in the opposite direction and was surprised to find that the Ka'bah too turned with the legs of the man. He tried it with another direction. The Ka'bah turned again in that direction. The humble man replied, "The Lord is enshrined everywhere and in all directions. There is no place where the Ka'bah is not."

There are several very important words in the Upanishads that are confusing to the first-time or a foreign reader. It is necessary to understand them to know the thoughts of the higher knowledge or wisdom of the Upanishads. They are Brahman, Brahmanas, Brahma, brahmin and Atman. The word Brahman is the unseen and unborn God of the Upanishads and used synonymously for Atman as well. The Brahman is the universal expression and the same is used in beings for the soul. The Brahmanas are textbooks, which describe the sacrifices and legends. The word brahmin is used for a priest who conducts large or small family sacrifices and rituals. The word Brahma is one of the Gods of Trinity – Brahma, Vishnu and Shiva. He is a creator of the universe. The word Atman is used for breath – Soul, Self, Prana, Purusha.

I will be failing in my duty if I do not mention a few names that are part of this work, involved directly or indirectly. Prem Narain Prem and Nirmal Kumar Jain have been very close to me for the last 50 years and have fashioned my ideas in life. Dr Krishna Khandelwal encouraged me to get my research published. Miss Sunita Sardiwal (MSc) and her family helped me in several ways to write this book. I have learnt a great deal in the company of Comille Sahiri and Padmanabhan, and his family. Lastly, my nephews Anand and Arun Agarwal, daughter Neelam Agarwal, and my grandson, Ajay Agarwal were very patient and cooperative while I wrote this book.

Mirgandra Agarwal

Contents

	Preface	vii
1.	Inspiration	1
2.	Gayatri	10
3.	Agni	20
4.	Aum	24
5.	Trinity	30
6.	Sacred Language of the Ancient Literature	38
7.	Introduction to Vedic Literature	44
8.	Vedas	56

- Rig Veda
- Sama Veda
- Yajur Veda
- Atharva Veda

9.	Brahmanas	74
10.	Upanishads	77
11.	Nirguna and Saguna Brahman	83

- Kena Upanishad
- Katha Upanishad
- Chandogya Upanishad

12.	Brihadaranyaka Upanishad	96

- Shvetashvatara Upanishad

- Mundaka, Prashna, Maitrayana & Manduka Upanishads
13. Sutras — 102
14. Puranas (Sanskrit Literature) — 106
15. Mahabharata — 109
16. Ramayana — 112
17. Panchatantra — 115

  Epilogue — 121

Inspiration

Reason is used to justify the human actions and activities. How will we justify a miracle and natural phenomenon? It is the sphere of inspiration.

Little or nothing has been said, heard, written and understood on the subject of inspiration which is of vital importance to the human race, as it is the exclusive gift of God to man. All the major religions of the world are silent on this subject, except Vedic literature that was conceived and composed in the true spirit of inspiration. Though the spirit of inspiration may exist in other religions yet it has failed miserably to affect mankind directly in a systematic and organised manner. Therefore, the contribution of the Vedas is unique in the history of mankind, for it has awakened man to distinguish between truth and untruth above all – also oneness with the Universal Self. The spirit of inspiration has existed at every step, in every ritual, in every chant and in the length and breadth of the Vedic literature.

It is not just a single prophet, holy place, idea that is responsible for the growth of the Vedic thought in the land of the Vedas. One in all and all in One is the heart and soul of the Vedas. From the Vedic times down to the present, the sun, the moon, the snow peak mountains, rivers, trees, etc., all have contributed to the development of social and religious thoughts of the Vedas. I dare say that an Aryan mind is the most scientific mind to understand and analyse the truth, and is real in its original and pure form. The sages and seers of the Vedas had discovered the par-excellence of this thought in their pure consciousness where every part of the nature, from a ferocious tiger to a poisonous snake, and from a saint to a sinner, played an equal part in the scheme of the universe. It has made the Aryan society love, respect and worship rivers, stones, trees and all the facets of creation. They not only love but also include them in their prayers, and make them a part of their devotion as they all have existence, and existence is truth. We have become seekers of individual destinies and ignored the destinies of the other human beings. All the great souls of the Vedas were children of love and inspiration, who had realised this truth in their meditation and contemplation.

In every age the *Gurukul* as an agency existed to impart knowledge to the children of successive generations in the land of Bharat. The teachers of these *Gurukuls* were fully equipped to develop the right qualities in children so they could understand the difference between the real and the unreal. Very often they used to declare, "Teachers are here to teach as well as to inspire." These teachers acquired inspiration and wisdom during meditation and contemplation. They understood that the main function of the teachers was to inspire their pupils by their sheer bearing, richness of behaviour, beauty of heart, strength of character and application of judgement. These would help to command the respect of their pupils and, above all, their storehouse of inspiration would make their students proud of being disciples of such teachers. The pupils would endeavour to reach towards the same or higher heights than their teachers, like Arjuna, Karna, Shankara, etc. In these Gurukuls teachers would dismiss their pupils with the following injunction, "Tell the truth; do your duty; do not neglect truth, duty, health, honour, prosperity; honour your mother as God; honour your father as God; and give alms in true spirit. When in doubt, follow the judgement of tried authority." It is true to assume that Vedic literature can be grasped without the knowledge and understanding of Sanskrit, but cannot be comprehended in the absence of a guru. A guru is one of the two essential ingredients of the Vedic tradition. The literal meaning of the Upanishads is to convey the same importance of the guru, i.e., to sit at the feet of the guru. The guru can also be compared to a lighted candle that ignites the soul of the disciple.

Life is useless if we are not inspired, as inspiration is the essence of life. Inspiration brings a dead man alive and a living man to the state of higher understanding and consciousness of social, spiritual and natural phenomena. In inspiration we develop our inner-self to such a level where distinction of the inner and outer, spirit and matter disappear, and reaches to perfection where one begins to feel that our Self is the same as in others. Those who have the flames of inspiration can stir the fire of great achievements in others. The Vedas were revealed to the rishis when they were in a state of inspiration, and the composition of the Vedas were the inspired achievement which shows the path of love, truth, higher knowledge and wisdom to all mankind.

In modern materialistic society our minds are attracted and occupied on hundreds of things. Several uncontrolled impulses rush into the brain and disturb the equilibrium and concentration. The function of inspiration is to check and bring the mind under control so that we can concentrate and contemplate towards certain goals to achieve brilliance and excellence for the benefit of the humanity. The whole subject of inspiration as an instrument of acquiring knowledge is a study of Raja Yoga in the Vedantic philosophy.

There are three instruments of knowledge in the Vedantic philosophy: instinct, reason and inspiration. Instinct is an immediate and urgent response of any situation by man or an animal. All the creatures in the animal kingdom react on the basis of instinct. Instinct does not involve any intelligence or thinking in the act. It is an involuntary action that originates in the mind to deal with the momentary situation based on fear or hunger. Sometimes, daring acts have been accomplished based on instinct that are not possible under normal circumstances by a normal being. The problem with instinct is that it cannot comprehend the whole situation, and only relates to the particular moment or situation. Therefore, it is a very rudimentary instrument of knowledge, as the sphere of action is limited, and choices are not available to act in a different way. It is only a solution of the immediate problem and not the long-term aim. The other drawback is that it cannot create anything or cannot change anything. Instinct is not part of progress or growth which is the ultimate objective of man and society.

The second instrument of knowledge is reason, and it is highly developed in man. Reason is the greatest attribute of man, and without reason man's action can be treated as illogical and wrong. Rational man learns and acts with the help of reason. Reason is used to justify human actions and activities. Generally, reason is the product of intelligence and used in artificial situations and activities that fall under the purview of human sphere. When we build a bridge over a river we justify it by the reason to cross the river, or when we punish a criminal we justify it by the reason to protect society.

Reason can also harm men and societies. The terrible destruction of persons and property during a war is justified in the name of freedom and peace. In fact, reason is also an inadequate instrument of knowledge as human action is limited. Essentially, knowledge is experience that we gain from ideas, acts and objects. In knowledge we divide, disseminate, compare, measure, categorise and make choices and create capacities. Thus, we create opposites in knowledge that exist only in relation with each other. Good exists in relation with bad. Justice exists in relation with injustice, etc. They are all opposites created by our knowledge of intellectual estimates. If there is no evil we will not talk about virtue. If there is no darkness we will not talk about light. If there is no wrong we will not discuss about right. A natural phenomenon cannot be justified by reason, and reality cannot be realised on the basis of reason. To justify the natural phenomenon man requires a higher instrument of knowledge than reason. For example, why does the sun rise in the east? Why do we have order in the universe? Why is day followed by night? These are the natural phenomena that cannot be explained by reason alone.

Very often, reason as an instrument of knowledge is also insufficient to operate, as it cannot get him very far. If you try to reason too far and too hard then it can bring about confusion, and reason becomes unreasonable. Take, for instance, what is matter? That which acts upon force. What is force? That which acts upon matter.

Take another example, between water and ice. Ice is formed of water under certain a temperature. One idea depends on another, and another depends on the third.

There is another philosophical metaphor. What is mind? It does not matter. What is matter? Never mind. Therefore a stage comes when you find a barrier before reason beyond which reasoning can go no farther. Either reason becomes a bad reason or it will work in riddles and form a circle from where you cannot escape.

Philip Sidney's saying will be most appropriate for this form of instrument of knowledge, "Reason cannot show itself more reasonable than to stop reasoning on things which are above reason." The Aryan mind does not hold this view and searches for the higher instrument beyond reason that is inspiration. Therefore, reason is also an inadequate instrument of knowledge as the sphere of human action is limited and cannot justify things that are beyond reason. For an average man reasonable action is the correct way to deal with normal things. Where extraordinary things are concerned, such as truth and reality, reason is not enough, and for this we need something extraordinary, an instrument of knowledge that is inspiration.

Moreover, knowledge acquired by the help of reason gives an understanding about the nature of physical objects, ideas or thoughts, and they are changeable. So these cannot be the criteria of reality or truth as they are changeless. Such knowledge is only a technique and not a goal, and brings a change of man and not in the man.

There is another element that should be understood regarding the relationship between reason and inspiration. Reason is the understanding and comprehension of the finite parts, whereas inspiration is the understanding of the real and whole. In other words, reason is the knowledge of the seen and known through the sense-objects like body, mind and intellect, whereas inspiration is the higher knowledge of the unknown and unseen. In inspiration, One in all and all in One is realised. Inspiration neither rejects nor contradicts reason but goes beyond reason where differences of opposites are united into higher knowledge or wisdom. Though reason has achieved great things yet its failures are greater for mankind. In reason we exalt and glorify human achievements but not the powers to use them for the unity and happiness of mankind.

Inspiration is the cause of freedom and reason is the condition of the bondage. Inspiration rises out of the soul in the quietness of prayers, meditation and contemplation.

Gandhi was inspired at midnight on 6 June 1893 in the waiting room of the railway station in South Africa in the solitude to find the answers of the human failures and their irrational justification. Moses was inspired in the solitude of the Mount of Sinai to redeem mankind from false values and beliefs. Buddha was enlightened in deep meditation under a tree to redeem man from worldly desires and ignorance. Jesus was inspired in the prayers, and Mohammed had seen Angels for the unity of his fellow Meccans in meditation and contemplation on the hills of Mecca.

This suggests that there must be some other instrument of knowledge beyond reason that is called inspiration. The things which reason cannot deliver or are unable to be delivered are accomplished by inspiration. Vedic literature declares that man cannot achieve victory through knowledge of reason alone, and he needs something which takes him beyond knowledge. In inspiration man pierces the frontiers of reason and justification, and acts sublime towards greater and higher goals for the eternal happiness of the whole mankind and beyond.

There are two kinds of knowledge, mediate and immediate or direct knowledge. To experience the mediate knowledge man requires both subject and object as they can be obtained through the instrument of sense objects, i.e., body, mind and intellect. Mediate knowledge is limited and conditioned which is changeable. Such knowledge should have form, action and thought.

Immediate or direct knowledge is that for which no action, no form or thought is required, and no instrument is necessary to experience it. It is the real and permanent knowledge. To know and experience the sun man does not need to light a candle. Inspiration is an immediate knowledge and develops "objectless awareness". It is the knowledge without properties and capacities. In inspiration we discover this immediate knowledge with the help of meditation and contemplation. It is not the result of any action and activity or the product of something else. The veil of ignorance is removed in inspiration and begins to realise One in all and all in One.

To know the nature of things you have to go beyond things, which is supernatural. To know the nature of the limit you have to go beyond the limit that is limitless. To know the nature of time you have to go beyond time that is timeless. To know the nature of finite one has to go beyond the finite that is infinite. Supernatural, limitless, timeless, infinite, etc. are beyond the comprehension of the sense-objects and mind. They are not objects, actions or activities that can be comprehended. They are the very subjects that comprehend all objects. Limitless or changeless has no form or shape, and no qualities or capacities, therefore it cannot be defined in terms of existence or non-existence. All things and happenings have existence. If these existence are taken off then nothing exists. The snake in the rope and the ghost in the post are mental phenomena arising out of misapprehension of the intellect that have defined boundaries. Secondly, change is always present in the changeless, and limit always exists in the limitless. Therefore, changeless or infinite does not mean the end of change or finite but goes beyond it.

There are dozens of well known examples in Vedic literature to explain such differences between finite and infinite or change and changeless. One such example is the space and the pot. The space enclosed in the pot is limited and conditioned by the wall of the pot. The space outside the pot is infinite, and the total space of the universe is conditioned by nothing. If the pot is broken, the pot space becomes one with the total space of the universe. In fact, the pot space was never separate from the total space while the pot existed. The existence of the pot space is only an illusion conditioned by the mud walls of the pot. Similarly, infinite is never separate from the finite even when finite existed in the infinite. These are conditioned by the sense-objects. In brief, the immediate knowledge gives us inspiration and visions of reality that is the basis of oneness or unity with the rest of the universe. Victory of one depends upon the defeat of the other. Success of one depends upon the failure of the other. Development of one depends upon the decay of the other. Virtue of the one depends upon the evil of the other. There is nothing like this in inspiration as all mankind shares in inspiration and the fruits of inspiration. None is the loser and everyone is the winner in the race of enlightenment, growth and self-realisation.

Gayatri

In prayer, subject and object are different; in mantra subject and object coincide into one.

The most sacred *Gayatri* of the *Rig Veda* is a prayer of prayers and *mantra* of *mantras*. When a lion appears in the forest, the rest of the animals disappear. When a king appears at the court, the rest of the audience bow down to the king in respect. The same is true with the sacred *Gayatri*. When it is chanted, the rest of the prayers and *mantras* occupy the rear seat in the Vedic religion. It is a prayer as well as mantra at the same time.

The chanting of and meditation on *Gayatri* awaken the soul for unfolding the mysteries of nature, which leads to the birth of inspiration and vision. Inspiration cannot be acquired or learned by reading, learning and experience. It only flashes through meditation, contemplation and devotion.

Recorded and non-recorded history provides the evidence that great souls have achieved spiritual consciousness in prayer, meditation and devotion.

Chanting helps us to grow in greatness, to discover the sublime in us and to recognise the divine possibilities in us. Knowledge gives us power; love gives us understanding of unity with the other and the *Gayatri* stimulates our intelligence and thought which go beyond power, time, space and motion. It dispels darkness and gives birth of a new man to understand the whole truth.

It appears that the *Gayatri* verse is addressed to God Savitr (ancient or pre-Aryan name of sun) who is the pre-Vedic aspect of sun, the stimulator and instigator of thought and intelligence. Like Savitr, the Vedas retain many pre-Vedic names of sun, e.g., Dhatr, Tratr and Savitr.

The word *mantra* is derived from Sanskrit root 'manana', i.e., *chintan* or thinking with deep meditation. In the chanting of the *Gayatri mantra* one concentrates on imagination, reasoning and movement of the mind to the adorable glory of the God, Savitr. When meditation reaches the peak one realises inspiration and vision. Chanting and utterance draw thoughts away from the worldly objects, and develops pointedness, which is the foundation of the inspiration.

Repetition is central to the concentration, which assists one to understand the reality, the truth and the absolute. It is correct to say that repetition is not conducive to rational or scientific knowledge, as it is the knowledge of the parts and not the whole. In the realm of higher knowledge we search for the whole and not the part. Scientific knowledge is objective and derived from the outer senses or physical world and unhelpful to the greater good of the whole mankind.

In the Vedas, 'Goddess' is described by various names such as devotion, religious emotions and spiritual feelings. The paramount importance and supreme position of the *Gayatri mantra* owes to the intimate religious emotions as a thing essentially divine. The sacred words are felt to be a kind of uplifting spiritual essence. The *mantra* becomes the symbol of holy utterances and holy thought. In sacred utterance we feel the sweetness and loving desire of the Supreme Being, and we reciprocate its feelings. In a famous hymn of the *Rig Veda*, 'Vach' (holy speech) is represented as the champion and upholder of the gods and its accompanied boons. The importance of chanting is so great in the Vedic thought that *Sama Veda* is called the Veda of chanting, holy utterance or music.

The sacred *Gayatri* is also a prayer. The word 'prayer' is derived from the English word 'petition'. Since creation man is born weak and imperfect, and above all, is surrounded by fear and insecurity. To overcome fear and insecurity man filed petitions in the court of Supreme Authority believing that there was some power that was regulating this physical world. For petitions man conceived and composed hymns or verses, describing the glory and greatness of God, and the helplessness of the poor self before the mighty natural forces. Therefore, the word 'prayer' is linked or associated with petition. In fact, it was the beginning of the science of religion, which consists of chanting or utterance of holy emotions and religious performance or religious activities. Religious performances and activities consist of offerings, sacrifices, *havans* and festivals. In Vedic religion, chanting is used in a wider sense than in other religions.

It is necessity which teaches man to pray. Everyone wants success—a trader wants profits, an enemy wants victory over another, a blind man wants eyesight, and a sick wants a healthy body. When the immediate needs of man are threatened then man prays in the hope that some help will turn up from invisible hands. Sometimes men pledge to offer something or pay a visit to a holy shrine of personal gods, if their prayers are answered. Such prayers are called conditional, when man makes a bow on the accomplishment of his desire. These conditional prayers are not mentioned in the Vedas and have been included in the Aryan religion in the post-Vedic era. They were very common in Greece at the time of Alexander and he brought these practices with him. With the cohesion of both cultures the Indians had adopted them in the religion. These conditional prayers are as valid as spontaneous, and have the same effect upon the deities. At times, these conditional prayers can be stronger than the spontaneous, depending upon the intensity and conviction of the devotees. Conditional prayers do not produce the spiritual consciousness or religious awareness in man, and so does not give birth to the inspiration and vision. It only effects the material well being of the individual.

In general, prayers are offered for material gains, few are offered for remission of sins and good moral conduct. Sometimes, man offers prayers for the protection of evil and unforeseen calamity. There are family prayers, which are offered to the health, prosperity and welfare of the family members. Occasionally, prayers are offered for progress and happiness of the society and the country. These prayers were very common in ancient Greece as a city or Poli was the unit of society. The Greeks were not famous for religious genius, and religious beliefs were useful for political purposes. Devotion to the city or state filled the spiritual bankruptcy of the Greek people and their psyche. It is a fact of history that Greece produced the greatest and most famous philosophers in the world, whom we envy even today, and they had contributed greatly towards rationalism, humanism and patriotism. They failed to develop the concept of religious forces based on spirit and soul. In spite of great intellectual traditions the Greek religion died and disappeared from the earth as it was based on the false adherence of religious patriotism. Greek philosophers failed to reconcile the individual religious needs of the soul. In the seventh century, Islam was inspired by these philosophers as well as the fear of conversion of the Arabian society into Christianity which made Islam a socio-political religion based on the unity of the Arabian people. In fact, the basic need of an individual is to develop the awareness towards all human beings and not only for the few that help to discover the Supreme within them. In the Vedic literature the *Gayatri* prayer recognises the paramount importance of the individual and enforces man's belief in the possibilities of the divine in him.

There is not much difference between prayer and *mantra* as both are the same in substance and essence. In prayer, man concentrates on the external ideal that is located outside him whereas in a *mantra* he concentrates on the internal forces to realise and develop the divinity within. In prayer, man adores an ideal object and it can be anything, and surrenders himself completely to the object. When an adoring man contemplates his ideal object he is filled with vision and inspiration. *Mantra* is a concentration of mind on a definite point till he finds that he has developed the powers to realise the truth and reality. Prayer involves adoration and *mantra* involves devotion. Prayer is objective and *mantra* is subjective. Devotion is the solemn mood of the soul, and adoration is the surrender of the self to the ideal object.

There are spontaneous and obligatory prayers. Obligatory prayers are prescribed by prophets and sages or by holy books. Spontaneous prayers are born of devotion towards the Supreme for surrender, irrespective of the consequences. They are not imposed from outside or superiors, and are the result of free will of man who has harnessed his spiritual needs towards the soul or God. Man who neglects the obligatory prayers is liable to be treated as a sinner or non-believer. Spontaneous prayers do not involve any such stigma. The contents of the obligatory prayers do not involve petitions, and only confess the greatness of God as well as praise His powers.

The contents of the spontaneous prayers range from petitions to moral values and every conceivable blessing. Obligatory prayers are rich in spiritual depth. In daily routine these prayers become thoughtless words and a mechanical process that lacks spiritual emotions or feelings though revealing religious depth and purity. A praying man does not obey his heart, but the external compulsion of the law, the fear of punishment and the hope of reward to go into heaven allure him. This fear of punishment and external compulsion deny the flowering of the soul, which blocks the birth of vision and inspiration.

Ordinarily, prayers and *mantras* celebrate the actions and powers of gods, and invoke their help for material gains, moral virtues and spiritual awareness. These are always uttered and chanted in verse. On the other hand religious performances or activities are conducted in prose. Poetry originates from the heart and prose from the mind. The source of religious poetry is the holy emotions and spiritual feelings. The source of religious activities is the heart, which wants to impress God by its activities and actions. Poetry is devotion while prose is reason. Poetry is vision and inspiration, and prose is knowledge derived from the past. Poetry is nature, and prose is non-nature. Poetry is the colour of society, and prose is the labour of society. Poetry is the food of the soul, and prose is the nourishment of the mind. In poetry man raises himself to a higher level, and in prose man remains at the earthly level.

Gods accept poetry, music and a devout mind as well as the value put upon them. The *Rig Veda* explains the great importance of the prayer in the following verse:

Prayers go by the path of the divine order to God,

Prayer born of the yore in the heaven,

Eagerly chanted in the holy assembly.

The *Gayatri mantra* is addressed to God Savitr—an aspect of the sun who is regarded as the source and inspirer of the cosmos. The sun is the immediate source of light, and expresses the nature of divinity much better than any other deity. It is the foremost visible manifestation of divine power. The *Rig Veda* describes Savitr as the promoter and giver of life on earth. The *sun* is the soul of all that moves or stands and exists in the universe. The sun is the eye of the sky as well as the eye of the whole world that looks upon the deeds of men and rouses them into action. The sun is also the divine priest of the gods. He prolongs the powers of men and drives away sickness, disease and evils.

This universal prayer is open to all men and women, high or low, and to all the people of different faiths. The *Gayatri* prayer asks us to seek truth fearlessly with single-minded devotion, meditation and concentration. It assumes the faith in the strength of the human soul. The prayer requires us not to lose faith in life but to endeavour to find the true self and lead life on the highest plane of human inspiration. The prayer suggests that our bodies are the temples of divine existence, and the heart is the deity of this temple. The soul is the true manifestation of the sun, which resides in the body. *Mantra* has the inherent quality of material manifestation of vision and inspiration. It is a universal prayer to the people of all faiths. Other religions make a single jacket and place it before society, and it must fit all members, irrespective of their sizes and measurement.

The effect and influence of the *Gayatri* was so great in ancient times that it travelled far and wide and as far as Greece. The Greek philosophers, Thales, Empedacles, Anaxagoras, Demecritus and Plato undertook journeys into oriental countries and acquired Indian ideas on Persian soil. Pythagoras and Plato visited Egypt and learnt Indian ideas from Egyptian priests. The historical possibilities that Greek philosophers and their thoughts were influenced by India through the medium of Persia are well-established facts. It is mentioned in Greek literature that this prayer influenced Socrates, and every morning he addressed his prayers to the sun. In another place, Plato in his tenth book of laws describes that Greeks showed reverence to the rising and setting sun, as *Usha* and *Sandhya* are the goddesses of the Vedas.

Similarly the *Gayatri* prayer is chanted in the morning, noon and in the evening. During the invasion and conquest of India, Alexander came into contact with holy men of India that puzzled him. It was the result of supreme and sublime force of the Vedic philosophy. Behind the invasion of India it was his deep longing to see the spiritual side of this country, which knew the truth better than anybody else in the world, and this thought was famous in Greece. He learnt this from his great master Aristotle.

Prayers are the soul and heart of every religion in the world. A non-praying man is considered to be a religiously dead man. Prayer is like blood, which circulates in the religious life of every man. In prayer man rises to the heaven and heaven comes to earth. The miracle of prayer does not lie in praying but in the mysterious contact between man and God, which enables man to perform miracles. Prayer is a miracle of miracles. Every prayer is turning man to a higher Being to whom he opens his heart with reverence, adoration and devotion. This Being is not an ordinary human but a superhuman Divine. A man who prays feels that he is very close to God just as a child is to his mother. It is in the meditation and contemplation of the prayer that he experiences direct contact with God and believes he speaks with Him. Immediately present before Him he has intercourse with God. The miracle of prayer does not lie in the accomplishment of the prayer but in the contact between mortal and divine spirit. The powers of praying are so great that a faint heart becomes a heart of steel, a feeble body climbs up the mountains, and a deaf man begins to hear. Prayer draws the great God into the smallest heart of men. In prayer the highest and the lowest come together at a place, which is consciousness of unity of God and man. In brief, prayer is a great wonder, which daily brings God in the heart of praying man. It is the light of all lights and the power of all powers. The power of prayer is so great that even an inattentive and unthinking prayer is not considered to be unholy and impious.

The *Gayatri* can be understood in different meanings and aspects. Prayer is devotion and sister of Faith, which occupies the status of a deity. Probably goddess Gayatri springs from this idea as a goddess. The sense behind this idea is that the sacred words and thoughts are divine. It fulfils all those attributes, which pleases gods. Prayer takes affect in accordance with *rta*, i.e., Cosmic Order. The sun is placed in the sky in obedience to the *rta*, and represents the concept of Universal Order. Harmony and righteousness as God Savitr is an aspect of sun and represents life in a being.

Another view of the *Gayatri* is that it comes from the Sanskrit word 'gai' which means to sing, and suggests that the *Gayatri* from the start was intended to be sung without melody or in ordinary poetry. The *Sama Veda* adopted the *Gayatri* stanza from the *Rig Veda*, and added a few syllables at the beginning, middle and end, i.e., *om, hai, im, sat*, etc., so that it could be sung with melody.

The third view of the *Gayatri* is that there is a metre of the *Rig Veda* called *Gayatri* and two-fifth hymns of the *Rig Veda* are of the *Gayatri* metre. Every metre of the *Gayatri* consists of three feet of eight syllables each. The *Gayatri* prayer of the *Rig Veda* is in this metre.

Aum is the primordial creative sound representing Brahman. *Bhur Bhuvah Svah* represents the three worlds—earth, atmosphere and heaven.

Tat savitr varneyum bhargo devasya dheemahe—adoration of the glory, splendour and grace that radiate from divine light and illuminate three world.

Dhiyo Yo Nah Prachodayat—prayer for liberation for thoroughly awakening of the light of the universal intelligence.

One who meditates and contemplates on the one foot of the *Gayatri* gives birth to a vision and inspiration and inherits the three world—earth, heaven and atmosphere—which go beyond time. One who knows and understands the second foot of the *Gayatri* inherits wisdom and higher knowledge of the three Vedas. One who chants and prays with religious emotions and spiritual feelings the third foot of the *Gayatri* conquers the breath. The breath or *prana* is supposed to be God Savitr and represents life in the Being. All the gods are good and kind. They do not thwart the requests or petition of man that comes with his prayer. Reciprocity becomes an accepted principle of the gods. The greatest attribute of a prayer is to help man to fall in silence. Silence or stillness is the key which lays open the heart to realise the mysteries of the universe.

The object of the sacred *Gayatri* is to show that we have nothing to gain, nothing to achieve and nothing to conquer but ourselves; that we possess everything within us. Subsequently he shines by his own light as the sun shines by its own light to lighten the world. The other aim is for us not to trust the external objects, which are the projections of the conditioned mind and the sources of illusion. We do not go to the burning house empty handed and without adequate preparations to extinguish the fire. The chanting and meditation of the *Gayatri* is the preparation to extinguish the fire of the body. We cannot construct a new house at the site of a burnt house unless we demolish and clean the site of the old house. The chanting and meditation is a way to demolish the fears of man.

Agni

The grandeur, greatness and influence of Agni can be measured in terms of space that he occupies in the *Rig Veda*. Out of the total 1,028 hymns in the ten books of the *Rig Veda* about 200 hymns are devoted to Agni alone, roughly a little less than for Indra for whom a quarter of hymns have been addressed in the whole of the *Rig Veda*.

There are three powerful and important reasons responsible for Agni to occupy such a high office and status in the world of gods. First, he brings prosperity and happiness to the homes of his votaries and worshippers who ask him to be present in rituals, ceremonies, sacrifices and other occasions. Secondly, he produces eloquence in himself and others who worship and honour him on occasions of religious as well as social and national importance. Thirdly, the greatest of all activities of Agni is that he produces and helps to conceive vision and inspiration, feelings and unity among those who are hosts or *yajmans* and men who join and share the *havans* and *agnihotras* for personal, family, community and national cause. This is the secret of Agni for the success, prosperity, wealth and inspiration among the worshippers.

In the Vedas, Agni has been raised to the status of a *devata*, who is instrumental in the conception of inspiration and vision. The importance of Agni is so great in our Vedas or *Sanatana Dharma* that no sacred or religious activity is complete and performed without Agni. He is involved at the sacred occasions in the family, in the temples or in the *yajnas* and *havans*.

Therefore, it is necessary and essential that he should be present in all our sacred functions in one form or another. The Sanskrit word 'Agni' seems to be related and synonymous with the Latin word 'ignis', the Greek God 'Ouranos', which carries a similar meaning as Agni in the Vedas.

We distinguish Agni as domestic and sacred in the Vedic literature. In the domestic sense, Agni is a father, mother, friend, guide and philosopher and belongs to all mankind. Agni dislikes no one, and is kind to all people, irrespective of caste, creed, race and religion. In this sense Agni gives us light and shows the right path in the darkness of night. In the sacred sense he is a *devata,* and worship is centred round him, and we pay our respect and reverence to him. At the beginning of the Vedic era it seems people gathered around a fire for their offerings of food and prayers to be passed on to other gods. We address and communicate with gods only through Agni. Man invokes gods and communicates his feelings, emotions and desires to gods with the help of Agni. Therefore, Agni is a messenger between men and gods, and fulfils a very high mission, which cannot be desecrated or insulted by any mean office or motive.

Agni is a mediator and through him we have our intercourse with gods regularly. Agni conveys the feelings and desires of the devotees to the gods. For this we offer principally ghee, curd or sweets during *havans* and *agnihotras.* Thus, Agni acts as a bridge between the two worlds—earth and heaven. It is a bridge of the mortals of the physical world and the gods of the heavenly world. In return whatever gods grant or bestow to the people in the form of boons and blessings Agni passes on to the worshippers. Agni is a very easily accessible *devata* who can be called any time and anywhere to communicate and to invoke gods with a little ghee, a lump of cotton, oblations and wood. The holy smoke which comes out from the sacred fire is to purify our feelings and emotions as well as the climate of the congregations and be ready to render inspirations to all those who share him with sincere and honest feelings and emotions. Due to his good, kind and sacred nature Agni is held in very high esteem and revered by all other gods. They never deny any request of Agni on behalf of the devotees. Agni does not like impurity, and so he destroys it at the very first opportunity.

In the *Yajur Veda* Agni has been described in three different forms based on functions. In the first reference he is an eater of raw flesh. This stage materialises when a building or a house is on fire, destroying property and burning men alive. In the second reference Agni is an eater of the dead corpses. This happens when we burn our dead to ashes to be scattered in the holy waters of the rivers. In the third reference he is in the form of a sacrificial Agni, when we offer our oblations, etc., and invoke the gods for our desires to be fulfilled during *havans* and *agnihotras*.

Agni has unlimited virtues, and it is believed that he does not make mistakes. If he errs in any fashion or manner he has the power and capacity to correct the error. Therefore, he is a *devata* who possesses all wisdom, and knows the past, present and future. He befriends his votaries and defeats his enemies as well. He has the power to remit sins and to avert the anger of Varuna. The *Yajur Veda* elevates Agni as the messenger to the gods, carrying any request made by the worshippers to be fulfilled. In *Taittiriya Upanishad,* Agni is not a messenger but the path that leads to the gods.

Agni provides awareness, consciousness, vision and inspiration to those who share and participate in the *havan* and *agnihotras*. These four qualities are the steps leading to the transformation of our existence. Agni provides this transformation only through the sacrificial fire for men who sincerely and faithfully believe in the mission and miracles, as he burns himself for the prosperity and happiness of others.

Agni is produced through the friction of two sticks, which is the Vedic process of invoking him. These two sticks represent the parents of Agni, the upper stick being deemed the male and the lower the female. Therefore, Agni is their child and has been given life by them.

The most important of the terrestrial deities is Agni. The bodily parts of him have a clear connection with the phenomenon of terrestrial fire, mainly in its sacrificial aspect. He is sharp and shining, with golden iron teeth, and burning jaws. The tongue and limbs of Agni are his flames. He eats and chews the forest with sharp teeth. He is driven by the wind and rushes through the wood. He also invades the forests and shaves its head as a barber does. His flames are like the roaring waves of the sea. The birds are terrified by the noise of Agni. The two sticks are his parents, producing him as a newborn baby who is hard to catch. From the dry wood he is born alive.

Agni is also called 'waking at dawn' as it is lit every morning for the sacrifice. He is old as well as the youngest god and termed ancient and young. He is regarded as having a triple character, born in the air, in the water and in the heaven. He is also a trinity of the sun, wind and fire, and regarded as the trinity of Brahma, Vishnu and Shiva. He has become a compulsory part of the sacrifice of the Vedas and Brahmanas. Agni is lit in many places and spots, and is the same everywhere. He is immortal and lives among mortals on earth. The term 'Grahyapati' is frequently applied to Agni. He is also as great a priest as Indra is a great warrior, mentioned in the *Rig Veda*. He destroys the enemies of his worshippers, like lightning destroys a tree. He grants boons and blessings to his worshippers just as Indra grants victory, power and glory.

In India, since the arrival of alien culture, Agni has nearly disappeared from many homes. During the Vedic era Agni was always present in the homes and Gurukuls where pupils used to learn in front of *agnihotras* that inspired them and filled them with great vision and joy.

Aum

In the *Yoga Sutra,* the great Vedic scholar, Patanjali, describes the word 'Ishwara' as *Aum*. Repetition of this name and meditation upon its meaning is 'aradhana', to realise God. Vedic sages did not refer to it as sound, but as a concept of the divine mind. The syllable *Aum* is the mother of all sounds.

Mantras are flowers of Vedic literature, and honey is hidden in the faith and devotion of the individual. Faith and devotion increase the concentration, which is the technique to obtain true knowledge of the Self. It gives power to the meditator to discriminate between the real and the unreal, between the spirit and the matter, and both are transcended into inspiration and realisation of the Self. Thus the individual crosses the river over this bridge of finite and infinite without sufferings.

The syllable *Aum* is a *mantra,* which should be chanted or meditated upon for a short duration of time to control the mind. The word *mantra* comes from Sanskrit roots "man" or "mind". Chanting or meditating of the sacred syllable allows consciousness to ride over the sea of the mind and directly affects one's attitude, emotions and thinking. It calms the mind and raises the vibration of the meditator, attuning him to the divine ground of existence, which is the condition of inspiration. In another meaning, *mantra* is a tool or instrument for stilling the mind. It is believed that the mind is like the trunk of the elephant. If an elephant is given a small stick to hold in its trunk, it will hold it steadily losing all the interests in other objects. It is the same with *mantra,* which gives the restless mind something to hold on to, quieting it by focusing awareness on one place. Therefore, chanting or meditation of *mantras,* prayers and *bhajans* controls the thinking process of the mind, and does not allow any disturbance to the concentration if it is done with faith and devotion. It is chanting and meditation that help the mind to remain vacant and silent. When the mind is silenced then the intuitive mode of consciousness begins to produce extraordinary awareness and inspiration.

The word *Aum* is holy and pure, and contains three letters of the English language. It is the most sacred symbol of the Vedas and Upanishad*s,* and begins with instructions to concentrate on this symbol. *Aum* represents the original sound of creation. In every religion in the world, when the natural phenomena or cosmic forces are associated with gods and personified, they become divine. Therefore, the symbol *Aum* is an expression of the divine in the form of sound. Chanting of this symbol means to share and to commune with the divinity.

The word *Aum* transcends the doctrine of trinity and duality into the Absolute or God. Modern physics has also proved that unification of opposites can be found at subatomic level when motion and stillness, sound and vibrations are transcended into a single entity. Matter is continuous and discontinuous; particles are destructible and indestructible; force and matter or waves and water are all different aspects of the same phenomenon. The force, which causes the motion in the matter, is not outside the object but is a latent property of the matter. Therefore, the soul inside the body is inherent like energy in matter or clay in a pot.

The syllable *Aum* is a symbol of the Supreme, and it cannot be realised without prayer and meditation. The chanting of *Aum* involves prayer and meditation, as speech is the essence of the Self that consists of two characteristics—sweetness and rhythm—along with sacredness. Prayer is a kind of submission to the external object; meditation is the exercise which involves the attention and concentration of the highest order. When meditation reaches the end without any distraction then the vision is conceived and inspiration is born.

Usually such inspirations are called moments of awakening or enlightenment. All the great souls of history, from Vyas to Vivekananda, have experienced such moments of inspiration in their lives. The noble quality of inspiration is that it does not depend on power and status. Every individual is capable of experiencing the flower of vision, and the fruits of inspiration will grow in him.

It is a fact that one who knows the truth becomes truth himself, and if inspiration is in man then he can inspire others. The *Maitiri Upanishad* refers to *Aum* as a symbol of sun and sung in the praise and worship of the gods. Consequently, an inspired man becomes like the sun and shows the light to others, thus becoming an agent of their transformation. According to the *Shvetashtara Upanishad* Agni exists all the time in wood, and is not perceived until one stick is rubbed against the other. The Self is like Agni; it is realised in the body by meditation on the sound syllable *Aum*. Let your body be the stick that is rubbed against it. Thus you will have inspiration and find God within, Who is hidden within the body as fire is hidden in the wood. The *Kaivalya Upanishad* also states that the mind may be compared to a fire stick, the syllable *Aum* with the other. When rubbed together and by repeating the sacred syllable and meditating on Brahman (God), the flames of inspirations will be kindled in your heart and all impurities will be burnt away. The *Mundaka Upanishad* refers to the significance of the syllable *Aum* by timelessness. The symbol *Aum* has no beginning and no end. One who has known and meditated upon *Aum* has resolved all dualities and trinities.

According to the *Mandukya Upanishad Aum* is referred to as Self. It has three aspects and the fourth is indefinable. The first aspect of the self is *Aum*. He is a universal person in his physical nature only of external objects. In this aspect the person is an enjoyer of the pleasures of the senses. In the second aspect the Self is a universal person, and, in this state the person is dreaming and conscious of his dreams. In the third aspect the Self is a universal person in the dreamless sleep, meaning he is without desire. The fourth state of the Self is not subjective or objective, or relative knowledge. It is pure unitary consciousness where awareness of the world and multiplicity is completely obliterated. It is one without the second. It is invisible and unutterable and beyond mind. Whosoever knows *Aum*, the Self becomes the Self.

In the *Mundaka Upanishad Aum* has been described as a bow, the Self as an arrow and Brahman as a target. In utterance and meditation one fixes one's attention and concentration on the target Brahman. The success of the marksman (Self) depends upon the practice of the arrow on the target. The Self or arrow can hit the target successfully provided it has enough practice in the form of single-minded meditation. The *Aitareya Brahmana* states that *Aum* consists of three letters which represent the consciousness. 'A' represents the consciousness in the state of walking, 'U' represents the consciousness in the state of sleep and 'M' represents the consciousness in the state of dreaming. These three stages of consciousness bring reality nearer to the developed soul. Further, the symbol *Aum* represents the essence of the Vedas and the universe. According to the *Taittiriya Upanishad* a person who recites and chants *Aum* with faith and devotion can make sun and Varuna gods friendly and ready to help him. This is the secret of *Aum*.

In the *Katha Upanishad* the syllable *Aum* is described as Brahman. This syllable is the Supreme. He who knows this syllable obtains all his desires of knowing the Supreme. It is the strongest support and the highest symbol. One who knows this is respected as a knower of Brahman. The Self, whose symbol is *Aum*, is the omniscient Lord. He is not born and does not die. He is neither cause nor effect. This ancient one is unborn, imperishable and eternal. Though the body is to be destroyed, he is not killed.

In the *Prashana Upanishad* the significance of *Aum* has been explained to Satyakama by his master Pippalada as follows, "The syllable Aum", when it is not fully understood, does not lead beyond mortality. When the meaning and substance are fully understood and meditation is rightly directed, man is freed from fear, whether he be awake, dreaming, or sleeping the dreamless sleep. Thus he attains the Supreme. By virtue of a little understanding of *Aum* a man returns to earth after death; by greater understanding he attains to the celestial sphere; by virtue of full and complete understanding he reaches to the stage of Brahman, the fearless and the immortal state.

In brief, the chant of *Aum* is a prayer to God in the form of sound, as the *pooja* of the image is an expression of devotion to God. The chant of *Aum* encourages you to engage in prayer and end up in meditation. Inspiration is the child of prayer and meditation upon *Aum*. Understanding of the eternal reality and knowledge of the Self is the reward of the chanting.

There are three vehicles of the Self, which transport him in the world of sense-objects: body, mind and intellect. The function of the body is to engage continuously in the activities of the sense gratification, which is subject to change, decay and death. The function of the mind is to develop the feelings and emotions towards those activities and objects which fall under the head of likes and dislikes. The function of the intellect is to develop the understanding of discrimination. To chant and meditate upon *Aum* is to keep mind and other sense-objects under control. It is the mind that projects and creates the attachment with objects, and brings the bondage and limited vision. The body gives the sorrows and sufferings in life. The intellect is capacity, which is limited and conditioned by the external forces. Every *mantra* allows you to concentrate on the Brahman and ultimate reality.

In the *Chandogya Upanishad* the syllable *Aum* is a syllable of permission. For whatever we permit anything, we say *Aum*. If *Aum* meant originally 'Yes' as *Amen* in Christianity, it may be assumed to have the same meaning, like *tat-sat* in Sanskrit.

There were two pre-Vedic words in use during the Vedic period: *avam* and *ayam*. *Avam* points to a distant object while *ayam* points to a nearer object. *Aum* may be a contraction from pre-Vedic *avam*, a distant object come closer to the Self or within the Self. In that case *avam* may become the affirmative particle of *Aum*.

In conclusion, meditation is one of the most important pillars of the Vedic literature for supreme knowledge, ultimate reality and oneness with God. There are two kinds of meditation: subjective and objective. In subjective meditation the Ideal is placed within oneself in the cave of the heart. The heart here does not refer to the physical organ which pumps the blood in the body but a lotus-like space formed when the mind is detached from the objects and the intellect becomes inert. The objective meditation is again classified into two categories—sound and form—associated with external objects. The reflection of the sound *Aum* in the mind becomes one with God. The sound ultimately leads the mind in silence. Thus the mind is freed from the heavy load of continuous and unending desires and temptations of the outside world of objects. As a result of self-control in meditation man is rewarded with vision and inspiration. From this we find that most of the *Upanishads* emphasised the importance of the *Aum* which plays a vital role in our religious life. Therefore, it should be meditated upon for the realisation of the Brahman within for inspiration.

Trinity

Trinity is creation, and God is the unity of creation.

The rishis of the *Rig Veda* envisaged the universe as three-domain—earth, heaven and air. This trinity is constantly expressed and implied in the Vedic literature, except in the *Upanishads*. The cornerstone of the Vedic literature is trinity. The Vedas and the Upanishads are centred on trinity and non-duality, and focus on ultimate reality of One. It appears that everything in the world is revolved around the doctrine of three or two, i.e., gods, men and demons; atmosphere, earth and sky; fire, water and earth; or soul and body; dark and light; truth and untruth; real and unreal. When water is drunk it divides into three: its coarse portion becomes urine, its middle portion becomes blood and its subtlest portion becomes breath. Ultimately all become united into One, like different rivers with different names unite with the ocean. Literally, the word trinity is applied and used in the Vedas. Here, it is called threefold knowledge, i.e., *traiya vidya* of the three Vedas: *Rig, Sama* and *Yajur Veda* (as sometimes *Sama* and *Yajur Vedas* are called and understood as attendants of the *Rig Veda*.). It is believed that *Atharva Veda* was incorporated at a latter date in the sacred knowledge of the Vedas. This may give you an idea of the majestic, regal grandeur and genius of the *Rig Veda*, which surveys the highest of the human intellect and depth, as well as the spiritual genius of the Aryans in the Vedic Age. Bloomfield in his book *The Religion of the Vedas* (1908) says, "*Rig Veda* is not only the most ancient literary monument of India but also is the most ancient literary document of the Indo-European people." It reveals a high level of civilisation among those who found in it the expression of their worship. Another great authority on the Vedic literature, Winternitz, in his book, *A history of Indian literature* (1927) also observes, "If we want to understand of our own culture, we must go to India, where the oldest literature is preserved."

These Vedas can be classified into three sections or *khandas*, which are called *Samhitas*, Brahmanas and Upanishads. It is just like an army of a nation in modern times, which consists of three sections: navy, air force and army.

In general, the Vedas signify the importance of three or the trinity of the 'P': poets, priests and praise. The poets of the Vedas are the greatest inspired rishis with sublime and the rarest insight. They conceived and compiled these hymns for the glory of gods and salvation of mankind. They also discovered in their hearts through meditation the bond between being and non-being, formed and formless, truth and untruth. Priests, who carried out rituals and ceremonies, displayed an astonishing and remarkable amount of courage and capacity to perform them with great care and precision. The correct performance of the *yajnas*, rituals and sacrifices are necessary components to obtain the desired benefits from gods and ceremonies. These priests were specialists in matters of etiquette and intercourse between the two worlds of gods and men. Praise was the central theme of these hymns by which they flattered gods and made them friendly, and encouraged them to grant boons and blessings to men who joined individually and collectively in ceremonies, rituals and sacrifices. In the hymns gods are praised for their heroic and heavenly qualities. Suggestions are also made in the hymns to reward the person who performs the rituals and ceremonies in their honour and respect.

Another doctrine of the trinity in the Vedas is the three 'S': *soma*, sacrifice and songs. *Soma* is the name of the plant out of which an intoxicating juice was prepared to please gods. The *soma* drink identified the immortality of gods in ancient mythology of Aryavarta. Book nine of the *Rig Veda* is devoted to glorify the *soma* drink, and is dedicated to Soma God. Sacrifice is the most vital link between men and gods, and is described in great detail in the Brahmanas. In the Vedic era there were no temples, and people used to assemble in an open place at the time of *yajnas* and sacrifices.

Besides the offerings of food and *soma* drink, sacrifices involve the recitation of *mantras* to invoke *devas* who come to attend the sacrifices. Sacred songs are important aspects of these hymns and verses. These are expressions, textures, and style of the literary genius and beauty of the Sanskrit language that encourage men to absorb themselves in the singing with undivided attention and concentration, which is the first stage of meditation. For this purpose, *Sama Veda* has a special kind of priest who sings these hymns in a particular musically chanting voice.

Again the doctrine of trinity is witnessed in the priesthood of the Vedic literature. These priests are classified into three categories. The priests of *Rig Veda* are called *Hotr* priests. They are simpler in attitude and organisation as compared to the priests of *Sama* and *Yajur Veda*. The priests of *Sama Veda* are called *Udgtr*, and sing hymns and prayers with a particular lilting chant so that they can create an effective atmosphere and environment during the ceremony. The priests of the *Yajur Veda* invented the sacrificial formulas. The priests of *Atharva* are called *Atharva*, which means fire priests or the priests of the fire people. The material of the *Atharva Veda* was the contemporary of the *Rig Veda* and even existed before the *Rig Veda*.

Sacrifice was the essence of the pre-Vedic times, and during the *Rig Veda* it became one of the three pillars of Aryan life in the land of Aryavarta. During *Yajur* and *Atharva Veda* it had occupied a dominant role in the sacred knowledge of the Vedas. Sacrifice in the Vedas is an imitation of the chief phenomena of the sky and the atmosphere. In every sacrifice of any kind gods are praised, entreated, encouraged to join, to share and to accept the offerings of the host. It is a notion that things wished or desired from the bottom of the heart may be made to materialise for the host who attends the sacrifice. In a large *yajna*, thousands of people assemble for the common cause, such as peace, victory in war, rain or prosperity of the nation, in a small *havan* when family and friends join for a special ceremony of health, family happiness, moving house, birth of a child, birthdays, etc. Fast, pilgrimage, charity, *tapasya, pooja,* listening to or chanting *mantras* are also forms of sacrifice, provided Agni is involved or present in these acts. Otherwise they are considered acts of kindness, pious, moral, and gesture of goodwill towards gods or fellowmen. It is only Agni who is friendly with the gods and men. So it requests gods to attend the ceremonies and sacrifices and asks to grant boons and blessings to the hosts. The other great virtue of the sacrifice is to raise awareness, concentration, meditation and purity of thoughts, minds and actions, which help to conceive the vision and birth of inspiration. Inspiration is the only higher knowledge that pierces the limits of time and space and goes beyond.

During the sacrifices and ceremonies our Vedic rishis used to ask surprise questions. Where is the sun at night? Where do the stars go at night? Why does not the sun fall down as neither is fastened nor supported to anything? Who is older—day or night? The answers to these questions were received during meditation so that they could perform great deeds and secure success of the highest order.

The doctrine of three 'D's has been proclaimed in the Vedas with the voice of thunder, which has never before been brought out by any religion, philosophy, morality or ethics: *damyatta, dayavan,* and *datta.*

Damyatta means self-control. Man must control his desires, liquidate his passions in the larger interests of truth, dissolve his pride and control his self-will. It will help him to win over himself.

Dayavan teaches us to have pity and be generous towards those who deserve it, as well to all fellow beings. It will develop the feeling of unity towards all human beings. We should grudge no one and forgive all. We may not have forgiven man's actions and activities. *Daya* is compassion and there is no virtue like compassion. Buddha was the embodiment of compassion.

Datta means freedom from greed, and helps those who are in need. Love others as you love yourself. Wealth can never be a source of immortality, measured by physical possessions. Man has to give it up for growth and well being of himself and his fellow-beings. In one of his sermons Lord Buddha said to his favourite disciple, Ananda, "Be like water which cleanses all without any distinction and does not make any discrimination between noble and ignoble, rich and poor, saint and sinner." Material things are used for the comforts of the body and senses, and love is felt in feelings, which must be converted into action and practice.

It would be better if this trinity can be presented in the original form. Gods, men and demons, all three descendants of the Prajapati, lived with him for a long time as students.

"Teach us, sir," said the gods. In reply Prajapati uttered one syllable, "Da." Then he said, "Have you understood?" They answered, "Yes, we have understood. You said to us, 'Damyamata'—be self-controlled." "Yes," agreed Prajapati, "you have understood."

"Teach us, sir," said the men. Prajapati uttered the same syllable "Da." Then he said, "Have you understood?" They answered, "Yes, we have understood, you said to us, 'Datta'—be charitable. "Yes," agreed Prajapati, "you have understood."

"Teach us, sir," said the demons. Prajapati uttered the same syllable "Da." Then he said, "Have you understood?" They said, "Yes, we have understood. You told us, 'Dayawan'—be compassionate." "Yes," agreed Prajapati, "you have understood."

The storm cloud thunders "Da: Da: Da—Be self-controlled. Be charitable, Be compassionate." This was the instruction of Prajapati to gods, men and demons.

In nature, birth and creation are sufferings, and the origin of sufferings is possession. Nature has order and system to perfect everything by itself, and pains or sufferings are the processes of perfection. Gandhi achieved nothing materially; Vivekananda did not make any progress in the material sense; Guru Nanak did not win wars; but they all recognised and realised the same soul they had in common with others. They were the children of love. When love enters in thoughts it becomes truth; when love manifests in the form of action it becomes righteousness; when feelings are saturated with love one becomes an apostle of peace. Oneness with the rest is the inherent virtue of love, which is manifested in all creations of nature from organic to inorganic. Love is the expression of the soul, and possession is the manifestation of the body and senses. In love, man experiences the understanding of the whole. India never idealised soldiers, statesmen, men of industry and science and not even poets and philosophers but those simple souls whose greatness lie in what they are and not what they do.

Christianity also preaches love and charity but with a difference—that it retains the identity of 'I' which is the basis of possession. As long as the human instinct of possession exists in man he cannot truly love others. In Christianity, man and God are two separate entities whereas the Vedas declare that the body is an illusion and the soul is a part of the Universal Soul.

Another trinity is the three 'Bs', according to the *Satpatha Brahmana*. Man has three births. One he gets from his parents, one he gets from sacrificial ceremonies and the last he obtains after death. The birth of inspiration appears in mind and soul, and brings the understanding of the higher process of nature in which one sees that the whole and individual is a part of the whole. It establishes the fundamental principle of the Vedas that soul and body are the two aspects of the same reality and both are the manifestations of the Universal Soul. To engage constantly in the activities of the body is a gross error, which is born out of desire and ignorance, and is a cause of grief and sorrow. Therefore, *Satpatha Brahmana* emphasises the importance of the ceremonies and rituals that can provide the opportunities to purify and prepare the ground for the inner self to give birth to vision and inspiration. This was the secret of the Vedic Aryans—that they attend, share and observe ceremonies from birth till death and even after death.

The doctrine of trinity has also been mentioned in the *Taittiriya Samhista*—of the three 'D's, i.e., debts of the Aryans. The first debt of the Aryans is to honour the sages and seers and to repay the debt by studying the Vedas, which will help them to transform the conscience. The second debt is to pay to the gods by sacrifices and *yajnas,* and the third debt is to pay to the ancestors by offerings in one form or another.

We find the trinity of three religions. One is the religion of prayers and sacrifices with devotion and faith. The second religion is the religion of Brahman and Atman of the Upanishads. The third religion is the religion of images and idols for all who are unable to follow the first two religions.

Another trinity of the Vedic literature is the trinity of mind, matter and *maya* (illusion). Maya unites the mind and matter. The understanding of the *maya* frees the mind from the matter, and it can be achieved through meditation. It will liberate the mind from the perishable and bondage of the matter, to become one with the Brahman and Atman.

Above all, the most important trinity of the Vedic literature is the unity of God, nature and man. The unity of these three is the highest task that he can set himself. This union with the Ultimate Reality is the ideal end of man's being. It can be realised through *jnana,* devotion and yoga. One cannot describe light to a blind man as it does not have sound, taste, form, or weight, nor can it be known by any process of analysis. Truth requires no authority than that which it contains within itself. Therefore, a blind man, through meditation, can comprehend light.

Sacred Language of the Ancient Literature

*Sanskrit is the mother, Pali and Prakrit are sisters,
and regional languages are children.*

The history of ancient literature is the story of the mental revolution and intellectual movement of India that continued from one generation to another and from one millennium to the next. Mental revolutions do not come all at once. India has proved by evidence of her continuous records that the higher and sublime thought has its beginning, middle and end. The theosophy of the Vedas is the beginning found in the hymns of the *Samhitas*, the middle in the Brahmanas and Upanishad*s*, and its final end in the philosophy of Sutras, Puranas, etc.

In the pre-Vedic era, India had developed the true national writing called Brahmi, and later all the letters of the alphabet originated from it. It was the most scientific language ever achieved by any nation in the world. There are 46 symbols or letters representing all the sounds, and arranged in a most scientific manner. The Western language has only 26 letters that do not represent all the sounds of the human speech, and have been arranged in a very unscientific and primitive order, used 3,000 years ago by Greeks. The West has reached the moon, surveyed the domain of the space and invented weapons of mass destruction, but failed to rectify or correct its own language on scientific lines. It appears that ten thousand years ago Indians had the most scientific stage of development and were the envy of the West. A philosopher of Europe at the beginning of the nineteenth century, Dugald Stewart wrote an essay in which he tried to prove that Sanskrit language was a farce and forgery made by the priestly class of India. A Dublin professor supported the same view in 1838. Since colonialism began, it has become the psyche of the West to portray the virtues and progress of the third world in a negative manner.

India was the vast country against the small pockets of countries on the European soil. Therefore, it is natural to divide the country on geographical grounds into several divisions for the purpose of language and literature. We can distinguish two forms of Brahmi writings of the ancient India: southern and northern Brahmi. From the northern writings of Brahmi originated the groups of northern scripts called nagari or Devanagari. All the northern languages of India like Hindi, Bengali, Gujarati, Marathi, etc. originated from Devanagari script of Brahmi, and from the southern variety of Brahmi five languages—Telugu, Tamil, Malayalam, Kannada, etc. developed in south India. No one is sure when, how, who had developed these scripts of Brahmi. One thing is certain—that these languages existed in one form or another at the time of Vedic era, and spoken by the common population like the unlearned, women and traders, etc. The great grammarian, Panini (many centuries before the Christian era), documented that these languages existed before the Vedic age among the ordinary populace of India.

In India, before the Vedic age, oral tradition was in vogue, when the literature and sciences were taught or learned orally from a teacher or speaker. Even today, some poets and teachers follow the oral tradition, and wish their work be recited rather than read. They derive great pleasure in recitation as they ascertain the depth of their poetry from the responses of the listeners. Writing was developed at a later date, and written on palm leaf in India.

The intellectual and mental activity in the Vedic period was developed partly by the observance of the natural phenomena in poetry form, called *Samhitas*, and partly from the study of the abstract in the mixed form of poetry and prose. We can distinguish this intellectual activity of the Aryans in Vedic and Sanskrit languages.

The Vedic language of poetry was conceived and compiled into three phases of development. The first contains four Vedas, accompanied by rituals and sacrifices to the nature gods. Their strength, virtue and grace helped to sustain life on earth and personified these nature gods. Even today we carry out the phenomenon of personification in human beings for their virtues and services as well as their finer qualities. We personified Gandhi as a mahatma for his glorious virtues and services to the whole of mankind. We personified Vivekananda, Ramakrishna Paramahansa as swamis for the services and sacrifices they made for us. Who knows, after 500 years, we may personify them as Vedic gods? Christianity and other religions also personified humans as saints, like St. Peter and St. Paul. The personification of nature objects in the Vedas was unique not found anywhere with such intensity, devotion, faith and spiritual feelings of holiness.

The second phase of the development of Vedic language is the appearance of the Brahmanas, *Aranyakaras* and Upanishad*s* in prose. It consists of the development of legends, ritual science of the Brahmanas and speculative thought of the Upanishad*s*.

The third phase of development is the appearance of Sutras and Puranas in poetry form. The most significant part was that it discontinued with the prose of the Brahmanas and Upanishads. The ancient languages of India can also be distinguished as Vedic dialect and Sanskrit language. The Vedic dialect does not differ from Sanskrit in phonetic conditions, and remains exactly the same as the early Vedic, in conformity. The change in the Vedic dialect occurred mainly due to the regulating effects of grammarians, which were most powerful in ancient India than anywhere else in the world. They were the great pioneers and exponents of the development of the Sanskrit from the Vedic era. Three most famous names commanded the full authority on the Sanskrit language. They were Yaska, Panini and Patanjali. Vedic language was merged with Sanskrit by their efforts. In fact, this merger partly happened due to the successive losses of the literature and change in the vocabulary. The vocabulary of the Vedic era had undergone great reforms. The changes happened due to the addition of the new words from the language of the people of lower classes like farmer, traders, children and women, who used ordinary words in day-to-day activities rather the language of the sophisticated priestly class of Vedic literature. The old words had been refined and reinterpreted with the new meaning. Several words had also been borrowed from the popular vernacular speech.

The post-Vedic development is called the development of Sanskrit literature; it can also be divided into several phases. It consists of the appearance of the Puranas, the epics *Mahabharata, Ramayana,* fairy tales, fables, etc. It was followed by post-Sanskrit literature in the form of grammar, phonetics, astronomy, mathematics, medicine and law. The seeds of Sanskrit and post-Sanskrit languages can be traced in the Vedas and Brahmanas. Some of the post-Sanskrit literature cannot be subscribed religiously but bears the stamp of religious ends and purposes.

Around fourth century BC several changes occurred in Sanskrit literature that were responsible for the development of Pali and Prakrit languages. Buddha and his successive followers preached their messages in vernacular speech as well as in the language of the ordinary man, contrary to the language of the learned and the intellectuals. Therefore, all Buddhist literature was composed in the vernacular. It has brought us in relation of Sanskrit to the local vernacular languages. Consequently, most of the Sanskrit words were changed into vernacular dialects, like the Sanskrit word *Dharma* became *Dhamma*, *Sutra* became *Sutta*, and *Vidyut* became *Vijli* or *Vijju*.

Sanskrit was transformed into the vernacular language called Pali. Pali as a language was first used around third century BC in Sri Lanka. We find many inscriptions of the Ashoka reign written in this Pali script. The Pali script became the dialect of Sri Lanka. The region of Middle India used this dialect known by the name of Prakrit, though it was Pali. Generally, Jains had used Prakrit language about the same time for their literature. And some of the Jain literature had been written in Prakrit language. Later, they began to learn Sanskrit, and wrote their religious literature in Sanskrit as well. Thus we deduce that Pali was the western dialect and Prakrit was the eastern dialect of ancient India. Both originated from Sanskrit by local and regional variations. It is the same local and regional variations with the northern dialect of Brahmi called Sanskrit and the southern dialect called Telugu, Tamil, Malayalam, etc. of south India. These language variations caused continuous modifications of the local words, and extended the derivations in all the languages of India.

After the development of various languages we can easily distinguish the Vedic and Sanskrit literature in spirit, contents, form and style. It will be unjust and erroneous to speculate that Sanskrit appeared at the end of the Vedic literature. It was contemporary and running side by side with Vedic literature, and beginnings of it can be seen in the Vedas.

The spirit of the Vedas is largely devotional and religious. It was optimistic and promised a happy and hopeful life in the future. The Vedic language was not the natural language of the population of ancient India but was the scholastic dialect confined to the priestly class handed down from one generation to another within the priesthood. The spirit of Sanskrit was the idea of transmigration due to the knowledge of the Brahman. The knowledge of the Self is the real knowledge. It will not produce *Moksha* but is *Moksha* itself. In the Vedic literature the spirit to worship the outer gods or gods of nature was paramount as they helped us to continue our existence comfortably on earth. The gods of the Upanishads were Brahman and Atman who are neither created nor born, and not subject to the laws of time, space and causality. The Vedic hymns were conceived in poetry form of metrical stanzas of four lines, and developed in the residential areas and settlements of towns.

Sanskrit literature is in mixed prose and poetry form. Sanskrit poetry was also composed in metres but is different in the sense that they are in *shlokas* of two or four lines and more elaborate than that of the Vedic poetry. The style of Sanskrit literature is more artificial than the Vedic literature as the rules of grammar are applied, and language is regulated by grammar. Thus, classical poetry of Sanskrit is like a garden of flowers unlike Vedic poetry which is a like forest where trees grow at will. The contents of the Vedic poetry are largely hymns of praise and songs. The contents of Sanskrit literature include legends, higher knowledge, fairy tales, epics, plays, etc. In essence, Sanskrit literature resembles the earlier Vedic age, except that the Vedic language was the dialect of the aristocratic class.

Introduction to Vedic Literature

In general, the word 'Vedic' is used for holy, devotional and higher knowledge, designated 'sacred lore', a branch of sacred literature. The particular meaning of the word *Veda* is 'sacred book' of the eternal or timeless religion. There are certain words in the Vedic literature that cannot be translated into English, which could give the correct meaning of the word, such as religion, Atman, *dharma,* etc. To translate Atman as soul is misleading as soul means animal or living soul, perceptive or thinking soul. All these meanings are perishable or destructible, and Atman is eternal and non-perishable. Similarly, caste is a Portuguese word, and had been used by Portuguese sailors for the first time to stocks or division in 1613. Professor Paul Deussen, a famous authority on Vedic literature, says that it is misleading and has mischievous meaning. In fact, certain native words cannot be translated into a foreign language, which could convey the exact meaning of the word, and regular use is dangerous. It can easily be exploited by the vested interests as has always happened throughout Indian history. German philosophers always tried to use the Sanskrit word if they failed to find the proper word, such as Atman for soul, or *anubhava* for experience.

Moreover, any definite period of the evolution of the Vedic literature cannot be assigned, as chronology is conjectural and based on vague astronomical or entirely on internal evidence. Historical evidence cannot be subscribed to India, as she has no history before 500 BC. Ancient Indians never went to wars for survival or struggle for life as Persians, Greeks, Romans and Arabs. In ancient India, intellectual life was always dominated by natural or spiritual ideas. When the Greeks invaded northwest India at the end of fourth century BC India was already rich with a national culture of her own, unaffected by foreign pollution, whereas the Greeks, Romans and Arabs raided and destroyed the culture of the defeated countries, and bankrupted the intellectual life of the natives.

The ingenious word *Veda*, based on traditions and derived from the Sanskrit word *Vid*, which means 'to shine', refers to higher knowledge or sacred wisdom attained through a process of intuition, personal experience in the state of awakening and inspiration. To take a dip in the holy waters of the Vedas means spiritual adventure, fulfilment of man's dream and mission of life, a change in the consciousness, an inner revolution and change in the understanding of man. These Vedas do not give us faith, revelations, dogmas and theories as were given by other religions. The Vedas are a record of inspired wisdom.

Dogmas, doctrines as well as revelations are curses of religions. They produce authority among the believers. It may have been good in the past when there was little knowledge. But today, in this scientific age, they are outdated and a source of disharmony, conflict and disorder. Experience of the inner and outer self is best to bring transformation of the Self, and create peace and understanding on earth.

The religion based on the Vedas is called *Sanatana Dharma* (eternal or ageless). *Sanatana Dharma* reflects the belief of eternity. It is a spiritual expression from the heights of personal devotion to the heights of abstract philosophy. In a way the Vedas are the pillars of strength, a reservoir of our spiritual genius, an ocean of inspiration, single-minded concentration, courage and wisdom that will continue endlessly to show the path of progress, peace and prosperity as long as the sun shines in the east and sets in the west. Until now no nation in the world has been more unjustly treated than India and her people. Since independence it appears things have changed, and the time has come when India can chart out her own destiny to bring back her spiritual heights, political wisdom and economic progress on the map of the world, and thus occupy the same space and place as was in the Vedic times. Now in a free India, anyone who is willing and ready to take a leaf out of this mighty tree of knowledge shines like a star in the dark skies. There is old Chinese saying, "It is better to have too little in the present than too much, and to leave things undone rather than overdo them." According to this saying one may progress little but one is definite to go in the right direction just as the man who wants to go further and further east will end up in the west. The study and understanding of Vedic literature with the right attitude may help one to enjoy and discover the rich, vast and versatile experiences of the past, which can transform the present and build the future. It will not only enhance the intellectual horizon of the individual but may provide an opportunity to develop the inner strength which is the essence of human progress, thus transforming the outer personality on the right lines of the human behaviour.

The word "Hindu" or 'Hinduism' had never been used or mentioned in the Holy Scriptures or literature of ancient India. These scriptures that are the backbones of Vedic or *Sanatana* religion. The Holy Scriptures, literature or books, like the Vedas, Puranas and *Gita* have never used these words in any manner and style. In Persian language, 'S' is pronounced as 'H', and with the exchange of culture and migration of the Persians into India, the Persians who settled across the Sindu river in the land of Aryavarta, began to call the inhabitants as Sindu which sounded like Hindu. This was the origin of the label 'Hindu', and later foreigners who entered before, during and after the invasion of Alexander started using the word Hindu rather than Sindu or Aryan. Indoctrination and imposition of alien culture took away the purity and originality of the native people, and harmed the emotional integrity and unity.

Anything, which is adulterated, is the source of disharmony. To know and learn an alien culture and language is good for everyone and is a source of greater understanding about others, but to be influenced by them is unacceptable to the pure and original. It is the highest form of bankruptcy and degradation of man and society. In the literary history of Ireland, H. Hide has said, "It is what the British tried to do in Ireland. The children are taught, if nothing else, to be ashamed of their own parents, ashamed of their own nationality, ashamed of their own names." As offsprings of the great Aryan stock, we have gone one step further, and treated our ancestors with disdain, considering our literature and culture to be inferior to Western values. Anything Western appeals to our eyes and minds making it superior to our own. According to a great German philosopher, the hallmark of modern civilisation is corruption. The glory of a shopkeeper lies in tempting customers to buy everything attractive displayed in the windows without much concern for its utility value. The glory of a politician these days lies in corrupting a large number of future generations.

Purity is the panacea of peace and progress whereas corruption and adulteration are the signs of decline, decay and degradation. Indoctrination is the raw material for imitation, which is a sign of despair and shallowness of man and society. It pierces the culture and language in such a way that it becomes second nature for man to imitate others easily and unconsciously. Whenever language and culture are wounded by imitation and indoctrination, decay and decline beset societies. The great section of intelligentsia and elite of a country, and the electronic media and books use a divisive language, and imitate without considering the effect, influence and consequences upon the masses or upon the society, as they are educated and trained in foreign languages. This displays the backwardness or bankruptcy of their own, and a void of purity, originality and glorious past. To label man as a Jew, Hindu, Muslim or Christian is a cause of dissatisfaction and division, conflict and confrontation in the people and societies. Ninety per cent of the conflict, chaos, disorder, violence and communal disturbances have originated from labels in the present world. To read and listen repeatedly to false indoctrinations and grow up in such an atmosphere is not only indoctrination but an insult, even a sin, against the intelligence and wisdom of our seens. Those who use it may have long-term goals to keep alive the conflict and violence in the world. They may be using it unconsciously without realising the effects upon the people, but it creates waves.

Harmony and not disharmony, love and not hate, construction and not destruction should be the norm of man and the goal of culture of every society. This is the message that has been handed down generations from the Vedic era down to the present.

Our Vedas are the treasure houses of love and unity, and above all of universal laws as well as spirituality, which treat and prescribe whole mankind as one family. Different seers and sages discovered these laws in the Vedas at different times in the ancient Aryavarta. Those who discovered these universal laws were rishis and sages of commanding heights before whom we are nothing. We have learnt to fly to the moon, to cross the ocean, but forgotten to tread the earth. The message comes out from these Vedas to give voice to those who have no voice, to give faith to those who have no faith, to show truth to those who know no truth, to give courage to those who are timid, and to give inspiration to those who have no inspiration or vision.

Unfortunately, we know very little or nothing, and whatever we know is seen through the coloured glasses of other people. Moreover, we know very little about our Vedas, the original source, the reservoir and foundation of our spiritual existence and genius upon which the whole structure of our society is built. We never strive or endeavour seriously to know and understand this rich and vital heritage and knowledge of the non-creation and formless principles, which may help our children and us to formulate our present and future. In fact, we have no time to spend in such fruitless pursuits. Today is the foundation of yesterday, and today is the foundation of tomorrow as well. Monday is the foundation of Sunday as well as Tuesday. All the modern theories of physics, such as the quantum theory, reveals that the universe is interrelated and interconnected.

Religion is meaningless to gods and beasts alike. In the arrogance of power/money or in the ignorance of darkness one may not realise the need and necessity of the religion of the Vedas, as it does not disturb the centre of our equilibrium and routine in life. In essence, the Vedas and Upanishads are the very basis and fundamental necessity of permanent happiness, lasting peace and future growth. Directly, Vedic philosophy is the backbone of our moral order, and indirectly it moulds and transforms our consciousness and purifies our soul. It extends great strength to us to face the challenges and upheavals in life, and inspires us to perform and accomplish sublime thoughts and acts in life. For example, a historian views the Taj Mahal from a historical point of view; an architect views it with structural foundations as compared to the layman who views it as a beautiful building. In other words, knowing and learning the Vedic philosophy of the greatest dimensions alter the attitude and behaviour of man, which is beneficial and useful for the peace, progress, and growth of the people.

By nature, man is stereotyped, and moments of inspiration come in every man's life when he can accomplish great deeds. The wise and intelligent use inspiration in a positive and constructive manner to advance the interests of the whole society and uplift mankind, whereas the unwise and arrogant misuse their inspirations to the detriment of the society as well as themselves. Some men are inspired by their own contemplation and inner strength while others by external environment. All the great, sublime and unique achievements are accomplished in the state of inspiration by an individual or by society. Vedas are such sublime achievements and contribution of Aryans, which were evolved and compiled in the state of inspiration about ten thousand years ago. These Vedas do not belong to any particular faith, society, race or nation, but is the property of all mankind, like other scientific and technological achievements. The same can be applied to the spiritual science of the Vedas to make the world a happier place to live in instead of fostering hatred and violence among the different societies of the different faiths. The Vedas are full of wisdom and inspiration rather than punishment and obligation upon the believers such as fear of sin propounded in Christianity and hell in Islam.

Vedic India was the home of genius and a fertile land of vision and inspiration that lit the eternal lamp of truth for the advancement of higher knowledge and progress of truth. This lamp of truth was conceived and lighted entirely on the Indian soil without being touched or influenced by any foreign elements. Other nations were subject to foreign experiences and imports of ideas. The rishis of the Vedas were simple sons of nature and not the producers or manufacturers of the truth. They were merely recorders of spiritual experience realised in deep meditation and contemplation. Spiritual experiences are the direct communication with God as sweetness is the direct experience of testing the sugarcane and not based on hearsay. In spiritual experience, barriers between the self and the Universal Self drop away and we feel unity with the Supreme. It is such an experience in which feelings are merged, ideas melt away, boundaries are broken, and one reaches to the state of realisation and Self-consciousness.

In modern India, Sathya Sai Baba has come to remind us that Vedic India cannot be clouded, as the past lives in the present, and the present reflects the future, like a father lives in the son and the son is reflected in the grandson. Sathya Sai Baba has direct spiritual communication with God and is considered an incarnation of God. His message of truth, love and service brings back the Vedic inspiration in the modern world to be realised and practised by every human being on earth. When inspirations touch our soul we become divine; when they touch our heart we become saintly; and when they touch our conscience we become free from bondage. When they touch our intellect we realise and recognise the unity of all. Our ancestors of Vedic age produced divine saints and philosophers who brought truth to the earth and clothed them in spiritual feelings, purified them with fire of *agnihotras* or *havans,* arranged them with wisdom and decorated with experiences of meditation and contemplation for the enlightenment of all human beings. *Avidya* or ignorance failed to arrest their intellect; reason failed to condition their mind about truth, as they were free from attachment, and understood that the soul or spirit resides in the body. Material, moral and social temptations did not succeed in extinguishing the light of the lamp of truth as it was lit by nature itself. The truth, which comes from nature, is absolute and eternal contrary to the truth which comes from matter. They discovered in their spiritual experiences that natural truth cannot be destroyed though it can be clouded for some time or temporarily by illusion or *maya,* as the sun covered by clouds. They discovered in the silence of meditation, whatever comes from nature is absolute and eternal. It is the natural that becomes supernatural, just as a child becomes an adult and a river ends up in a ocean that forms the larger and higher entity. Natural and supernatural are two aspects of God as body and soul are two aspects of the Brahman.

Nature is movement and continuous, with no duality, nothing superior or inferior, great or small. All things in nature come into the world with a mission, and fulfil their mission quietly without asserting any authority, power and importance in their function. It is not attached with anything. After fulfilling their function they go back to their destination from where they originated. This is the universal law and order of the nature. One who understands this is an inspired man or realised soul. Realisation of this universal law is a great secret of peace, happiness and consciousness.

Nature does not know good or evil, right or wrong, justice or injustice. There is nothing moral, rational or social in nature as these are grouped together. In nature nothing is dependent on another or another dependent on the third. Everything in nature, from a tiny particle to a great mountain, and human beings, are free and independent as they function with their free will. The natural laws function in being and non-being, visible and invisible, or form and formless alike. Clouds are formed from a formless sky, and rain is the consequence of the natural law.

This nature was the vast temple of the Vedic Aryans and they did not invite their gods to dwell in the castles, temples, churches or mosques as the whole nature was the playground and resting place for their gods. They rightly believed that sky and earth was a union of husband and wife and whatever came between them were their children who must be loved and respected. So they blossomed to their full strength and realised the unity of all. Everything in nature, from bacteria to mountain, being and non-being, was a source of love and devotion to the

Aryans as they appeared with a mission and fulfilled their function without imposing any authority. They were all parts of the One and manifestation of the One in different forms and shapes. Form or shape was not important, as it was a medium to represent the unity of the universal law. In nature even a tiny atom is better than a human being as it obeys the laws of nature, whereas man, in his indolence and pride, disobeys the order and laws of nature.

An animal is wiser than man, for it fights and kills for fear and food only. The moment food is secured for the day and fear disappears from the life of an animal, it does not worry about the next meal and roams in the wild as a free being, living according to the laws of nature. On the contrary, man violates the laws of nature and tries to conquer her. In this process he learns to live unnaturally and attaches greater importance to the needs of the physical body over nature. Excessive attachment, storage and the accumulation of material objects for the body are responsible for his ignorance, which cloud his understanding and judgement about nature and soul. The futility of the body as well as the material objects have been exposed with the greatest clarity in the Upanishads. Therefore, failure to realise unity in nature hinders man's spiritual growth towards the Absolute. Our Vedic forefathers were the greatest thinkers of our race and the human society. For them the idea of God presupposed the idea of absolute unity with nature. They realised that the relationship between general and particular, between universal and specific were the expressions of the same Brahman, and both were the one, as particular was the manifestation of the general. Man cannot understand things which are human, unless he understands things which are natural or divine.

During the Vedic age, we know of no great teachers likes Plato or Kant. There was no university like the Harvard or Cambridge. There was no monastery like the Vatican or Mecca.

There was no prophet like Buddha, Jesus or Mohammed. There were no antique of coins, stupas or anything else except Vedic literature which was the result of their spiritual experiences. They had proved the truth, that our soul is a part of the Universal Soul. When Sathya Sai Baba produces a miracle he is claiming a truth—that the spirit or soul within us is mightier than the world of things. It is the spirit in man which is capable of producing miracles and not the phenomenal body. Therefore miracles are materialised by the spirit and not by the body. All the great masters of divinity in other religions caused miracles, and that is the manifestation of the spirit. When Jesus said, "Destroy this temple and I will raise it again," it signifies the power of the spirit. The human body is the material fact whereas the soul is a universal truth. God is the Universal Spirit who lives within us and outside us. If He does live within us then there is no need of God to us and if God lives outside, then there is a sense of worship. Such was the message and *mantra* of the Vedic seers, which was not only unique but also good enough to realise God.

India did not produce politicians who created division and conflict in the name of rule and administration. India did not produce generals who murdered millions and destroyed property in the name of democracy and freedom. India did not produce scientists who invented weapons of mass destruction in the name of scientific progress. All these men belong to history. History is the record of evils and cruelties of a few powerful men to exploit the masses for the benefit of the elite. On the contrary, India produced simple men of enlightened souls who were born to remove the veil of darkness and ignorance. For this they had gone through the process of grief and sorrow, pains and sufferings. Such men will always be born in the soil of India to uplift the masses.

Once there were two close friends (one was a believer in God and the other was a non-believer), talking about incarnations, prophets and *avatars*. The non-believer said to the believer, "Prophets and incarnations existed for thousands of years in history but man has not changed a little. There are still greed, authority, murder, violence, hate, war, jealousy, etc." The believer did not reply at that time. One morning, as they were walking through the streets of the city, they saw some filthy children playing in the dirt. The believer asked him, "How many years is it since soap was first invented or produced?"

The non-believer replied, "Hundreds of years ago."

The believer asked, "Why are these children still filthy?"

The non-believer said, "Because they do not use soap."

Believer: "Now, whose fault is it that they remain dirty?"

Non-believer: "The children."

Believer: "Why not the soap?"

Non-believer: "The children have to use soap to keep themselves clean."

Believer: "This is the same with prophets and incarnations. Man has to listen and follow the *avatars* and prophets in order to purify himself. The fault lies in men, not in the *avatars* and prophets."

Vedas

*Rig Veda is the Lord of the lords,
holy of the holiest, and sun among the countless stars in the sky.*

More than five millenniums before Christ, India was the epicentre of great intellectual and economic activities. Her Vedic literature was moulding the destiny of her people by discovering universal laws about soul and body. There is a unity in nature and everything is the manifestation of one God.

At a later date few agricultural tribes of neighbouring Persia (Iran) began to migrate from the Persian highlands to the north of India in search of economic prosperity and to improve the standard of living that was not possible in their own country, exactly in the same way as the Asians of today are migrating to Europe and America to improve their fortune. With the passage of time these tribes settled and integrated with the native population of India but retained their link with their mother country. It led to exchange of ideas and information about the Indian experiments with truth and God. It helped the native Persians to develop and to create a similar type of experiment in their own land. Therefore, it is truly believed that Persia exercised considerable influence over the development of Egyptian and Grecian thought in the later centuries.

We find many concepts of the Vedas in Persian literature, i.e., the concept of *rta* or Cosmic Order. The most important book of the Iranians is *Avesta* and it is sometimes believed that there is less difference between the Vedas and *Avesta* than the later epic *Mahabharata*. From Persia, Vedic thoughts spread to the wider world of Egypt and Greece as well as other civilisations.

At the end of the Vedic era, two thousand years before the birth of Christ, Vedic literature was canonised in the form of Vedic corpus. During this period the whole of India was inspired, producing two of the greatest men in the history of mankind—Buddha and Mahavira, founders of Buddhism and Jainism, respectively. These two religions were the product of Vedic literature and cannot be understood without the knowledge of the Vedas, as Vedic literature is the foundation upon which their superstructure was evolved.

Similarly, Christianity and Islam are the products of Greek thought, and cannot be understood without the prior knowledge of Greek thought and Jewish religion. Five hundred years before the birth of Christ, Alexandria was the centre and seat of art, culture and learning. Great philosophers of Greece, Persia and other countries used to meet there and exchange ideas. Thales was the first great philosopher of Greece who often used to visit Egypt and exchanged ideas with Egyptian priests. The doctrine of the Empedocles, "Nothing arises which has not existed before, and nothing existing can be destroyed," has its exact parallel in the Sankhya about the eternity and the indestructibility of matter. All these pointers give the impression that Indian thought was gaining ground in Greece before the birth of Christ.

The direct link between India and Greece can be traced to the sixth century before the birth of Christ. A Greek named Skylax is said to have travelled to India and navigated the Indus in 509 BC. Greek writers gathered all information from his travel accounts of India. Another Greek physician, Ktesias, learnt much from the Persians and was personally acquainted with the learned Indians. Alexander the Great was well informed about India before leaving Greece to conquer the world.

In Vedic literature, we find a gradual advance from the material to the spiritual, from the sensuous to the super-sensuous, from the human to the super human, and ultimately, find the divine in man himself. Man becomes divine when he is lifted above the level of the rational and social. Sir William Jones was appointed judge in 1773 in Bengal, India. He says, "It is impossible to read the Vedas or many fine compositions in it without believing that great masters of Greece like Pythagoras and Plato derived their sublime theories from the same foundation with the saints and sages of India." Schroeder, writing in an essay in 1884 (Leipzig), said that almost all the doctrines ascribed to Pythagorean were current in India as early as six century before Christ, and pronounced India to be the birthplace of Pythagoras's ideas.

David Frawley, a Vedic scholar, based his calculations on astronomical references in the *Rid Veda* and this fact takes creation even further back to the six to nine millennium. The other astronomical evidence proves that the earliest *Rig Veda* compositions date from at least six millennium years before the birth of Christ. Recently BBC television had shown a programme about the period of the *Rig Veda* in which it declared that the birth of Vedic era was about eight to ten millennium before the birth of Christ. German philosopher, A. Weber, wrote in his book, *History of Indian Literature* published in 1852, "The literature of India possesses generally for the most ancient literature in the world of which we possess written records and justify so." He did not try to give the determination of Vedic period. In fact, he explicitly declared any such attempt to prescribe the date and period of Indian Sanskrit literature was futile.

German philosophers have always been the most ardent and honest admirers of Vedic literature. Fredrick Schlegel says that early Indians possessed a true knowledge of God. All Vedic literature was filled with sentiments and expressions, noble, clear and serenely grand, deeply conceived and reverently expressed in any human language in which men have spoken to God. And again, even the loftiest philosophy of the Europeans, idealism of reason, as advanced and promulgated by Greeks, appears in comparison with the abundant light and vigour of oriental idealism like a feeble promethean spark in the full-moon blood of heavenly glories of noonday sun, faltering and ever ready to be extinguished. His brother, A.W. Schlegel, became the first professor of the Vedic literature in the West in 1818 in the University of Berlin.

When Max Muller began to publish for the first time the texts and commentaries of the *Rig Veda*, some interested parties argued that the Vedas were useless. The Vedas might do very well for Germans but not for Englishmen. Churchill once said, "Mahatma Gandhi is a half naked fakir," an arrogance of British psyche. Another German writer, Herman Hess, a Nobel Prize winner was the product of the Vedic literature and all his works were covered by Vedic philosophy.

The greatest among the historians of philosophy of France, Victor Cousin lecturing in Paris in 1828-1829 on the history of modern philosophy, spoke before the audience of two thousand gentlemen, "When we read with attention the poetical and philosophical monuments of the East, above all, those of India, which are beginning to spread in Europe, we discover many truths, and truths so profound, which make such a contrast with the meanness of the results at which the European genius has sometimes stopped, that we are constrained to bend the knee before the philosophy of the East and to see in this cradle of the human race the native land of the highest philosophy." The

English historian, Arnold Toynbee, observed, "It is already becoming clear that a chapter which had a western beginning will have an Indian ending. At this critical moment in human history of ours the only way of salvation for mankind is the Indian way." Will Durant, in the story of civilisation in 1935, states, "India will teach us the tolerance and gentleness of the mature mind, the calm of understanding spirit and unifying love for all."

'Aryan' is a Sanskrit word which means 'noble' or 'one who knows and understands the value of life'. There are several other English words, which carry the similar meaning as 'Aryan', like, respectful, sire, reverent, etc. So Arya Samaj becomes the community of the noble people. Max Muller, in his book, *Ancient History of Sanskrit Literature*, published in 1859, described that India was a land of philosophers. "Through the medium of these lines I want to wake you up and like to remind you to make your present worthy and future as glorious as was the past. I sing this hymn in your praise as Aryans used to sing the hymns in praise of gods in Vedas, 'O Indians, get up and rise, recognise your potentials, work hard and conceive a vision and inspiration so that your nation can be proud of you.' " Examine the greatness of the Aryan belief of the Vedas in the following sentence, "My soul is directing a path for me and your soul is directing the path for you. They are not the same but both are valid." It explicitly signifies that other religions may not necessarily follow the same route but they are all valid as long as they lead you to gods. So we must respect every other religion and their beliefs in the same way as we respect and love ours.

The four names of the Vedas do not coincide with the earlier names, as they came at a later date of the Vedic era. The earlier names refer to the different styles of composition as well as the contents of the texts of pre-Vedic literature. The *Rig Veda* is the oldest and most important canonical collection of the Vedic pantheon. The *Rig Veda* is the lord of lords, book of books, holy of the holiest and sun among the countless stars in the dark skies. The importance of the *Rig* can be viewed with four aspects in mind. Firstly, the vision of beauty has been described. Secondly, the power of deities are ready to shower favours on the devotees. Thirdly, the myths and legends have produced the literature of the greatest magnitude to civilisation. Myth is a phenomenon of nature as an act of divine or super-human but not as a result of any law. Legends are stories of heroic deeds and action of man or gods, and miraculous events with or without divine interference. In his address to the Asiatic Society of Bengal in 1786, Sir William Jones said, "Whatever be its antiquity, is a wonderful structure, more perfect than the Greeks, more copious than Latin, more refined than either." The religion of the *Rig* is the religion of the priestly class, and was running side by side with the *Atharva Veda* of the ordinary people of India. The *Rig Veda* has two fold interest: it belongs to the history of the world and to the spirit and soul of India. In the spirit of the world it takes us back to the times of which we have no records anywhere, only conjectures and guesses of the culture and civilisation. In the sense of the spirit and soul of India the whole superstructure of Indian thought, philosophy and culture is based on the *Rig*. The Vedas is not a single book like the Quran of Muslims, the Bible of Christians and Tripataka of Buddhists, but mental revolution arose and continued generations after generations. In mental revolutions the mind is awakened and interprets the old symbols in a new way suited to the contemporary society. The chief characteristic of this intellectual movement is not to disturb or shake the old beliefs of the ordinary men, but lead them to the new meaning so that it may build up a new society to suit the new conditions.

Rig Veda

There are 1,017 hymns and over a hundred thousand stanzas divided into ten books, and if the supplement is added in the *Rig Veda* the hymns add up to 1,028. In the *Rig Veda* gods are personified for their qualities and functions, not found and contained in moral beings of the earth. These qualities are power, beneficence and wisdom. The character of Vedic gods is moral to a limited extent, as they are true, honest, and not deceitful like men. Moral elevation in the *Rig* is not expressed but is the power and valour of the gods produced by prayers, sacrifices and offerings. In the Brahmanas sacrifices are represented as all-powerful, controlling not only gods but also the very process of nature.

The most important god mentioned in the *Rig* is Indra, and this can be judged by the space he has occupied in it. About a quarter of the hymns or 250 of the total hymns have been devoted to the praise of Indra. Indra is the god of thunder, conqueror of demons, drought or darkness. He is also the god of war, and is invoked to help during conflict with the enemy. He destroys the enemies of his worshippers. He also grants victory, power and glory. In the Brahmanas Indra was the chief god of heaven.

The next important god mentioned in the *Rig* is Agni. About 200 hymns, roughly one-fifth hymns, have been devoted to him. This has been described in detail in the chapter on Agni.

Varuna is another god mentioned in the *Rig* and is a great friend of Indra. He has played a more important role in the earlier sections of the *Rig*, and in the later sections Indra has become more important in the hymns. In these hymns Varuna surveys the sky, and is the upholder of moral order. The character of Varuna is described in the hymns of the *Rig* as follows. "By the law of Varuna heaven and earth is holding apart. He has made the wide path for the sun. He causes rivers to flow. By his ordinance the moon shines brightly, moves at night. He is the hater and punisher of falsehood. He frees man from sins committed in compulsion or free will."

Surya is also a very important god in the hymns of the *Rig*, and five aspects of the solar god have been mentioned.

Surya is one and the sole guardian of the universe. He is the sight of the whole world. All beings depend on him. He drives away diseases and evil dreams. A total of 11 hymns have been allocated to him in the *Rig*.

Gayatri or Savitr is another solar god, and 11 hymns have been devoted to him. He is the most powerful god with regard to the development of mind and intellect. Morning or evening repetition of this *mantra* is extremely beneficial to the mind and intellect.

Vishnu is another solar god, who is not as frequently invoked as Surya or Gayatri.

Usha is the only female god in the *Rig*, and a complete hymn has been devoted to her. She has also been celebrated in 20 other hymns, suggesting the importance of her in the life of human beings as well as animals. She removes the darkness of the night and gives rest and peace to man, and prepares him for a hard day's work. A man rises in the morning and sees the natural phenomenon of the glorious maiden Usha and sets forth for his prayers and sacrifices that would bring him wealth and comfort.

Rudra is another god mentioned in the *Rig*, and injurious features are attached to him. Three hymns are addressed to him. Marut is another god and the son of Rudra. He is the shoulder of young warriors and celebrated in three hymns in the *Rig*.

Prajapati is another god in the *Rig* and his name is repeatedly used in the Upanishad*s*. He has been referred to as the Lord of creatures in the tenth book of the *Rig*. Prajapati is regularly described in the *Atharva Veda*. In the *Sutra* he has been identified as Brahma, a god of the trinity—Brahma, Vishnu and Shiva. A deity of this name occurs in the oldest and latest part of the *Rig* as an abstract god.

Brihaspati is another god in the *Rig*, and referred to as the Lord of prayers and teacher of gods who come to him for learning and guidance.

Vedic literature is a religion of nature, so animals, forests, rivers, trees, insects play a great part in the mythology and religious conceptions of the Vedas.

The cow is most often mentioned in the *Rig*. In the *Atharva Veda* the worship of the cow is fully recognised and accepted. The *Satapatha Brahmana* enforces and anticipates the evil consequences of eating beef. It advises about avoiding eating beef at any cost.

The horse draws the cart of the gods, and so commands respect.

In the *Rig* the serpent is most important as an obnoxious animal. In other Vedas, the serpent is mentioned as semi-divine. In the *Atharva Veda* herbs and *mantras* are prescribed as antidotes to destroy the effects of the serpent bite. In the Sutras offerings are made to avoid the evil consequences and poison.

In the *Rig*, plants, water, rivers, mountains, heaven and earth are frequently invoked as divinities, and these are parts of the Vedic sacrifices and worship in one form or another. One whole hymn is addressed in praise of plants along with their healing powers. In the *Atharva* plants have become more important as they possess the power to cure diseases. Some plants like peepal and tulasi are recognised as holy. One whole hymn is also addressed and celebrated to forests. The plough is invoked in a few stanzas as they help to grow grains on which life is dependent.

Yama has been recognised as the king of the dead, and three hymns in the *Rig* have been addressed to him. There are many legends in the *Rig*, which have been developed in the Brahmanas. The owl and the pigeon have been mentioned occasionally as regular messengers of the king of the dead. The dog is used in the Rig Veda by the name of *vivasvat* as a regular messenger of Yama.

The most important concept of Brahman as an abstract god in the Upanishads has been used in the ninth book of the *Rig Veda*. The Brahman means devotion in the *Rig*, and has been developed in the Upanishads. The whole structure of higher knowledge of the Upanishads is based on this concept. In the *Rig* devotion bestows great benefit to the devotees by influencing and compelling gods in favour of worshippers.

Sama Veda

All the hymns of the *Sama Veda* are borrowed from the *Rig Veda*, except 75 that are independent and the original creation of the sages of the *Sama Veda*. Most of the stanzas are composed in *Gayatri* metre or strophes known as Pragati that are compounded of *Gayatri* and *Jagati* verse lines of the metre. In the hymns of the *Rig Veda* sages of the *Sama Veda* have introduced certain exclamatory syllables such as *sat, om, gai, im, hai,* etc. so that stanzas could be sung in melodies. The *Sama Veda* is mostly devoted to the worship of Indra. It has several *Samhitas* such as *Maitrayani, Taittiriya, Vajasaneyi,* etc. In Europe, for the first time it was fully edited by a German philosopher, Benfy, in 1848.

The chief and prominent characteristic of the *Sama Veda* is the shift of devotion to music and melody, from the prayers of the *Rig Veda*. Therefore, music becomes the fundamental thought and desire of the *Sama Veda*. The power of music has become so great in the minds of the *Sama* sages that they believed music influenced and compelled gods to do the will of the offering priest. Special priests called *Ugatr* or chanters sing the *mantras* or prayers on special ceremonies. Priests are trained to sing the *mantras* in melodies. For this reason it is called the Veda of music. Even stanzas that are subordinated to music, have been intended to be sung in melodies. It is the belief of the sages that music brings a special effect upon the deities who are there ready to grant boons and benefits to the worshipper. Music is the soul and food of gods as it circulates in the body like blood and stirs up the emotions. Even animals are intoxicated with the effects of the music.

Yajur Veda

The appearance of the *Yajur Veda* in the Vedic literature introduces a new development in the history of religion and social life from the ancient to the present. The stanzas or songs of the *Sama Veda* have been compiled for the application to sacrificial rituals only, i.e., one part of the ceremony. The stanzas of the *Yajur* supply formulas for the whole ceremony itself, and have become the central thought and desire. Their correct performance is all-important and necessary. The power of correct performance has become so great that it not only influences the deities but also controls the gods to do the will of the offering priest. Therefore, correct performance and formula for the whole ceremony is the main ingredient of the *Yajur*. The *Rig Veda* attaches its main focus on devotion to the prayers, the *Sama* attaches it to the music, and the *Yajur* associates devotion to the correct performance that became the cornerstone of the Vedas.

The history of religious and social development suggests that the gap between the *Rig* and *Yajur* may be a thousand years. During this time new ceremonies were developed for every occasion in ancient India. Hence, sages of the *Yajur Veda* composed new verses and stanzas for every type of ceremony. They borrowed nearly half of the stanzas of the *Yajur* from the

Rig, and the rest half are independent and original creation. The partial originality of the stanzas is the result of the growth of new ceremonies and extraordinary development of rituals in detail. There is no difference in style and language between the new hymns of the *Yajur* and those of the *Rig*. But the true spirit of the *Rig* is missing under the influence of continuous sacrifice and ritual control over nature. These ritual formulas of the *Yajur* are recognised having a magical effect rather than supernatural powers of the *Rig*. It has introduced the miraculous powers attached to the penance and asceticism among the priests and population. This element emphasises that purity of the body and behaviour of the priest is important. The priests and population undergo various kinds of holy routine before the ceremony. It means they should study, follow and observe the rules of the spiritual life and set an example to deities. Later, these practices were incorporated in every type of religious activities of Vedic religion as well as in Buddhism.

In the field of religion, the name of Prajapati appears frequently in the forefront as the head of the gods in the *Yajur* whereas the name of Prajapati is used only in the last and tenth book of the *Rig*. Secondly, Rudra in the *Rig* was recognised as injurious and evil, but in the *Yajur* he began to appear in the form of Shiva. Vishnu in the *Rig* is mentioned and not worshipped but in the *Yajur Veda* he occupies a more important position than in the *Rig*. The most important new development occurs in the form of demons called *asuras*, absent in the *Rig* and the *Sama*. The *asuras* appear as an evil group of people, opposed and constantly in conflict with the beneficial gods of the previous two Vedas. The conflict between the demons (*asuras*) and gods occupies a considerable part in the *Yajur* and the legends of the Brahmanas. The wives of the demons, called *apsaras*, occupy and play a considerable part in the post-Vedic mythology that has not been mentioned in any form and fashion in the *Rig*.

Atharva Veda

Patanjali, an ancient Indian philosopher and grammarian, expressed an opinion in his commentary, that the *Atharva Veda* was the leader and chief of all the Vedas. *Gopatha Brahmana* raises the status of the *Atharva* as the highest and greatest compilation of religious lore, and calls it *Brahma Veda*. From the history of the civilisation of India and the world's point of view it is more important than the *Rig,* as it deals with all the important aspects of human life, from religion, law, holy charm, medicine, astronomy, etc. As a religious lore it is recognised and accepted as the last Veda of the Vedic age but the contents run side-by-side with the religion of the three Vedas. Most of the contents were developed even earlier than the advent of the Vedic era. The spirit it breathes appears to be pre-historic and pre-Vedic.

The word *Atharva Veda* first appears in the *Griyha Sutra* as early as the *Rig Veda* and other *Samhitas* of the Vedas. The Puranas regularly mention about *Atharva Veda* in their own sacrificial rituals. In the *Mahabharata* the importance and valuable contribution of the *Atharva Veda* has been fully accepted and recognised by Vyasa.

The oldest name of this Veda is referred to as *Atharvangirash*. This is the compound word and formed from the two names of the ancient families of the priesthood. The Atharvan family is associated with the holy charms from generations and most versatile in other branches of the *Atharva Veda*. The Angirash family is attached with witchcraft and hostile spells from generations in ancient India. The name of Angirash is found in most Brahmanas and occurs in the Upanishad*s*.

The *Atharva Veda* is divided into 20 books and contains 730 hymns about 6,000 stanzas. Out of the 6,000 stanzas, 1,200 stanzas are derived from the tenth book of the *Rig Veda* and few others from nine books of the same Veda. Twelve hymns of the twentieth book of the *Atharva* have been taken without any alteration, and the rest of the hymns have been altered here and there to suit the purpose for which they have been employed. One complete hymn in the twentieth book has been addressed to Indra. The sixteenth and seventeenth books of the *Atharva Veda* are the shortest, containing only four and one hymn, respectively.

All the three Vedas are composed in poetry, and a major portion of the *Atharva Veda* has also been composed in poetry. Only one-sixth part of the *Atharva Veda* is compiled in prose, the language of the Brahmanas followed by it.

From the point of view of language, the *Atharva Veda* is compiled after the *Rig* and before the Brahmanas prose texts. As far as the vocabulary is concerned, popular words are not used in the previous three Vedas, and the *Atharva* has taken advantage, using the popular words to a remarkable degree of success in the composition. Therefore, it became more popular and accessible to the masses of ancient India, and was responsible for the development of other sciences like astrology, medicine, philology and astronomy in the post-Vedic period.

There are two kinds of charms and spells which have been described: auspicious and hostile. Among the auspicious charms, many *mantras* and prayers are for long life, sound health, freedom from illness. Another class of auspicious charms includes prayers for protection from dangers and unforeseen calamities, prosperity in the house and business. The third class of auspicious charms includes hymns to secure harmony and friendship, and ascendancy in conferences. Another group of auspicious charms includes *mantras* for the royal election of the heirs, restoration of an exiled king, attainment of glory in life, victory in battle, and for striking terror in the enemy camp. Given below is a specimen *mantra* for protection from danger and calamity:

> As at all times lightning strikes,
> Smites irresistibly the free,
> So gamesters with dice would,
> Beat irresistibly today.

There are hostile charms directed against diseases, demons and ghosts, and spells to cure fever, leprosy, jaundice, scrofula, cough, baldness, fractures and wounds, snake bites, poison, etc. These charms are carried out with the help and use of herbs. The herbs are the most important antidotes against hostile charms and spells. Experiments have been continuously carried out ever since in herbal medicine in the development of treatment of various illnesses. These charms have been recognised in the *Mahabharata* where herbs have been used for the cure of various illnesses and diseases. In ancient India charms and spells were in vogue and no hostile attitude was adopted against them as we find today.

The *Atharva Veda* also contains massive astronomical data. It was the first in the history of world civilisation to explain lunar divisions in the nineteenth book of the *Atharva Veda*. On the basis of astronomical data post-Vedic literature developed the science of astrology, which has been copied, borrowed and developed by Arabs and Europeans to exactness. Hence, the *Atharva Veda* is the oldest literary monument of great importance for the development of India in medicine, astronomy, astrology and other branches.

It was right time to establish a Vedic university in a Vedic village to advance the study of the *Atharva* literature with the cooperation of Germany, as most of the work outside India was carried out in German language. It had great potentials in the field of astronomy, astrology, medicine, grammar, philology and music. In astrology, the sun sign, Capricorn, rules India, and the ruler of Capricorn is planet Saturn. The planet Saturn is exalted, elevated and glorified in the sun sign of Libra, the seventh sign of the Zodiac.

Two great men of recent times were born under the sun sign Libra, Gandhi and Dr Abdul Kalam, in the month of October. India being Capricorn-exalted, and elevated by Gandhi's and Dr Kalam's, birth in this land, made enormous progress. The reported birth date of Dr Manmohan Singh is 26 September, and the sun falls on this day at 3 degrees in the Zodiac sign of Libra. Seventy-one years ago, the transiting Jupiter planet of expansion, progress and success elevated his sun in Libra. The planet of Saturn, the ruler of India, is exalted and glorified in the sign of Libra in the horoscopes of Gandhi, Dr Abdul Kalam and Dr Manmohan Singh. Astrological indicators suggest that he should go down in history as a great Prime Minister of India. Under his leadership India can make great progress in all areas of society that would put India as a great nation among the league of developed nations, or even higher. The Libran trio of Mahatma Gandhi, Dr Abdul Kalam and Dr Manmohan Singh will be remembered as responsible for inspirations for India making great strides in its development. The sun sign Aries rules England, and the ruler of Aries is Mars, exalted and elevated in the Capricorn, the tenth sign of the Zodiac. Aries England, exalted and elevated in the sign of Capricorn of India, made her empire in India. Astrologers also advised Britain to assign number 10 to the residence of English Prime Ministers. India can seek the advice of astrologers to assign number 7 to the address of Indian Primes Minister's residence, and this would elevate the status of future Prime Ministers.

Astrology is a science of "potentials and opportunities" hidden in signs and symbols of an individual's birth chart. History or epoch-making events do not occur frequently; such events put us on the path of success or failure as the case may be. It is the combination of the planets' position at birth; progression and transits set the motion into play, unseen by the native. The strength and weakness of one's life is determined at the time of birth in the chart. It is not a fortune-telling game, as most people believe it. One must remember that all people do not respond to the planetary influences alike. Circumstances, temperament and conditions vary with different people in society. For instance, a stroke that flattens clay has little effect upon a block of wood, nothing upon a stone, and it simply shakes the grass.

To quote a very interesting case study, Samuel Hemming and King George III of England were born at the same time on the same day, 4 June 1738. Both of them had a similar appearance, and their lives ran in close parallel on different levels according to their family background. Hemming inaugurated his steel and iron business on the same day that George III was crowned the King of England. Both were married on 8 September 1761, had the same number of children of the same sex, became ill and had accidents at the same time. Both died on 19 January 1820 of similar causes. It is possible to document dozens of such cases of relativity. It is evident from the study that family background plays a vital role in the life of an individual. I have a close relative who has planet Mars in the sign of Cancer at birth and it is exactly the same with his three sons. He sees the effect of this in life. (Exceptions and free will are there.)

It has been repeatedly explained in the book that scientific knowledge is not perfect as it is acquired by senses.

The research will open new channels to perfect the science of astrology by introducing the scientific year of 365 and a quarter days, rather 360 days in the year of Indian astrology based on the movement of the moon rather than the sun. Secondly, the scientific year of astrology varies with the transit of the sun, and begins on the 18th to 22nd day of the month when sun enters in the next sign, rather on the 14th day of every month in Indian astrology. Thirdly, there is no research of the three new planets discovered in recent centuries—Uranus, Neptune and Plato. Indian research can establish the properties and qualities of these new planets and apply the science to astrology. The Indian ayurvedic system of medicine has enormous potentials in the medical science that suits the conditions and circumstances of India. Research is needed in herbal medicine that can be developed to discover the treatment of new diseases like AIDS, cancer and strokes. In the nineteenth century Europeans had borrowed the operation of rhinoplasty or formation of the artificial nose from India through the Latin translation of the ayurvedic system of medicine.

In science the debt of Europe and the world to India has been greater than astrology and medicine. The Indians invented the numerical figures used all over the world. The influence of the decimal system cannot be comprehended and measured by human intellect. Modern India is fully equipped for the twenty-first century to accelerate scientific and technological development, and lead the world in computer sciences.

Brahmanas

The mental revolution of the Vedic poetry shifted to the prose of rituals and ceremonies that produced the massive literature of the Brahmanas in the Vedic age. They describe, explain and discuss the significance of the nature of things in general. They have produced different types of theological treatises, speculating their origin and importance of the whole Vedic process. They are called ritual textbooks. The main object of the Brahmanas is to explain the value of the ceremonies. Their contents can be classified under three heads: procedure (*vidhi*), explanation and philosophical discussions of the ritual. It took a long time to develop, just like the Vedas, as it passed from one generation to another.

The Brahmanas explain ceremonies on the one hand, and myth and legends on the other. These are responsible for the development of Sanskrit literature in the form of the Sutras, Puranas and the great epics. Every Veda and Upanishad has its own Brahmanas, and explains stories in detail. The *Rig Veda* has three most important Brahmanas: *Aitareya, Kaushitaki* and *Sankhayana.* These contain numerous myths and legends.

In the *Aitareya Brahmana* is a story of a king, Harishchandra, who was childless and bowed to the deity, Varuna. He prayed that if he should have a son, he would offer to sacrifice him. The king was blessed with a son but he deferred the fulfilment of his promise to sacrifice his son, Rohita. When the son, Rohita, grew up, Varuna pressed Harishchandra to perform the sacrifice of his son as promised. Rohita escaped to the forest and wandered about for six years. Varuna inflicted his father with a serious illness. King Harishchandra met a poor brahmin who agreed to sell his son for hundred cows as substitute for the sacrifice of his own son. Varuna agreed and said that the brahmin boy was worth more than a son of a kshatriya. When the sacrifice of the brahmin boy was to commence, the boy went on praying to various gods to save him from the sacrifice. The various gods listened to the prayers of the boy and King Harishchandra was restored to his normal health again.

Another legend of the *Rig Veda* traced the play *Urvasi* of Kalidasa, developed in the post-Sanskrit literature. There is another *Brahmana* of the *Chandogaya Upanishad* dealing with the ceremonies, relating to births and marriage prayers addressed to various divine beings. The soma books of *Brahmana* are devoted to the famous soma sacrifice and many legends. The last chapter of this *Brahmana* is intended to obviate the evil effects of various events. The prominent feature of Brahmanas of the *Sama Veda* is their mystical and secret speculation as well as identifying various kinds of *ragas* and chants with all kinds of terrestrial and celestial objects. Other Brahmanas are theosophical in character containing secret speculations about Brahman who appeared again and again in the Upanishads and the higher knowledge based on it. The *Satpatha Brahmana* of the *Rig Veda* describes the legend of Manu who came into possession of a small fish, which asked him to protect it from floods. This legend was developed in detail as the beginning of the creation of the universe in the Puranas.

After the *Brahmana* literature another development is of great importance the *Aranyakas* or forest books. These are the end part of the Brahmanas and have theosophical character. They do not give rules of performance of sacrifices and explanations like the Brahmanas, but supply the speculative teaching of the sacrificial religion. These works were supposed to be used by pious men who retired to the forest and no longer performed sacrifices as they had renounced the family life to record their experiences about God, truth and other celestial phenomena. They were intended to be communicated to the pupils by their teachers in the solitude of the forest instead of in the village or town. Moreover, it is also possible that certain sacred rites were performed in the seclusion of the forests where teachers and pupils meditated on the significance of these rites. There is not very much difference between the Brahmanas and the *Aranyakas*. In fact, they are a kind of transition to the higher knowledge of the Upanishads and form the concluding chapters of the Brahmanas.

Upanishads

Knower of God is higher than the worshipper of God (Deussen).

The first direct link of the Vedic and Sanskrit literature with Europe can be established in AD 1651 when a preacher, Abraham Roger, living in north Madras, translated the Indian poet, Bhartrihari, in Dutch language with the help of a local brahmin. It went unnoticed as Abraham translated it for his own pleasure, happiness and intellectual curiosity.

In AD 1640 the Mughal prince, Dara Shikoh, went to Kashmir for holidays and someone mentioned the brilliance of the Upanishads to him. After returning to Delhi the prince invited great Sanskrit scholars from Benaras to Delhi to translate the Upanishads in Persian. The Persian translation of the 50 Upanishads was published in 1657 under the title of *Oupnekhat*. Three years later his brother Aurangzeb, alleging that Dura Shikoh was a danger to the religion of the empire, put him to death. There was a lull for about a 100 years. In 1775, M. Gentil, a French resident in the court of Shuja-ud-da, sent the Persian translation of the Upanishads to a fellow traveller, du Perron, who took it to France. The Latin translation of the Upanishads was published in France under the title of *Ezour Vedam* that created a sensation and left a deep impression on the minds of the great French philosopher, Voltaire. The play of Kalidasa, *Shakuntala,* was published in Latin in 1789 and from Latin to German in 1791, by an Englishman, George Forester. It spread like fire and drew the attention and awakened the leading poets of Germany, like Goethe and Herder.

The Latin translation of *Ezour Vedam* was published in German in 1801-02. It is said that the German philosopher, Schopenhaur, had the Latin translation of the Upanishads on a table in his bedroom and before retiring to bed he performed his devotional reading from its pages. He writes, "Upanishads sooner or later would become the faith of the people. They are the products of the highest and greatest wisdom." He further states, "Upanishads are next to original and most rewarding reading possible in the world. It has been the solace of my life, it will be the solace of my death." In Paul Deussen's eye, "Upanishads are the fruits of the most profound insight that the world has ever known, almost super human thought whose authors can scarcely be imagined to have been mere men. The authors and thinkers of the Upanishads have obtained it with not the most scientific yet still the most intimate and immediate light upon the last secret of existence."

Indian thought of Vedic literature is the chapter of the greatest product of the human mind. The great Indian philosopher, Shankaracharya, says that man is like a plant. He grows, flourishes and at the end dies but not totally. For, as the plant, when dying, leaves behind its seed from which according to its quality a new plant grows, so man dying leaves his *karma.* It is without beginning and without end.

The characteristic of the Upanishads is the whole vision set towards God and it always fails to see him. Its long pilgrimage is to his feet and yet cannot overtake him. St Augustine similarly expresses the same views, that God is above every name that is named. The double aspect of God as One in whom all is lost and yet the One in whom all is found seems to be inexpressible only by asserting the failure of all expressions.

Another characteristic of the Upanishads is that they are intellectual and aristocratic, while popular devotion of the Vedas is emotional and devotional. The aim is in each case to obtain unity with God. In his manuscript written for university lecture to the students, Schopenhaur wrote, "The result of that which intends to present to you agree that knowledge is not the means of liberation but the liberation itself." He who has obtained the conviction, 'I am Brahman' (God), has reached with the knowledge that he is himself the totality of all, and he will not fear anything because there is nothing beyond him. He will not injure anybody nor injure himself. There is no means of attaining this knowledge, it comes by itself. The Upanishads have been described as a practice executed with knowledge.

The first religion is the religion of the Vedas in which gods are worshipped with devotion and prayers. The second religion is the religion of the Upanishads in which knowing or knowledge of God or Atman can be acquired through meditation, discrimination and contemplation, separating the imperishable from the perishable.

Both religions are not only complementary but are the same in essence. The seeds of this monumental thought were laid down in the ninth book of the *Rig Veda*, where sages used the word 'Brahman' for prayers and sacrifices. The word Brahman is also found in the *Atharva Veda*. The God of the Upanishads can be summed up in a single word, the universe is Brahman, and Brahman is the Atman. The greatest religion of the Upanishads begins where the religion of the other people are content with their doctrines and dogmas, not so with the Aryans who believe that the truth in man is in fact the ONE truth in all universe. There is one eternal truth and we are part of it. In the religion of the Upanishads Aryans have to forego worldly pleasures and earthly happiness, and suffer and renounce temporary comforts for redemption of the cycle of birth and death. The word 'Brahman' represents the cosmic principle, which pervades universally. 'Atman' is the psychological principle manifested in man.

In the Vedas, Brahman is ascribed as super-human or super-divine as a sacred magic formula or power by which man desires to influence divine beings or forces. The two words 'Atman' and 'Brahman', being used with exactly the same meaning as sacrifice, was conceived as superman in the Vedas. In the Upanishads this Brahman or sacred knowledge came to be called the first created being, Paramatman, and finally even to be made into a creative principle, the Cause of all existence.

The meaning of Atman is very simple and some derive it from the root, 'to breathe,' soul, self. Atman is psychological principle and freely used in Sanskrit, whose meaning is self and denotes one's own soul, one's own body, in contrast to the outside world, but most frequently the soul, the true self, in contrast to the body. These two are united in the philosophy of the Upanishads to become one.

In St. Petersburg Sanskrit dictionary we find Brahman explained as 'the devotion that appears as the craving and fullness of the soul'. According to Deussen, Brahman is the 'will of man' striving towards that which is sacred and divine.

The Upanishad is not a book or work of a single or hundreds of men. It is a system based upon a series of books written in different times, various locations, by hundreds of sages from one generation to another about the experiences of one truth, of Atman and Brahman. The eternal divine power Brahman is identical with Atman. This identity is the fundamental thought of the doctrine of the Upanishads.

Paul Deussen describes the Upanishads in three different meanings: secret words, secret texts and secret imports. Secret words denote the mysterious expressions or formulas intelligible only to the graduates. These contain secret rules for action and behaviour on the nature of Brahman, and do not apply for worship but meditation. Secondly, The Upanishads are books of the past containing the knowledge of the Brahman. Thirdly, he mentions secret imports in the sense that they are not the work of the priestly class, and have been contributed by other sections of the people of society, like kshatriyas, farmers, traders, maidservants and others in the Vedic literature.

The Upanishad is a compound containing three words: *upa-ni-shad*. It originated from the root 'shad', meaning 'sit', proceeded by two prepositions *ni*, meaning down, and *upa*, meaning near. So it expresses the idea of a session or assembly of pupils sitting down near their teacher to listen to his instructions. Shankaracharya and other Indian philosophers describe the word that derived from the root 'shad' which means destruction. They merely intended to destroy ignorance and passion by means of higher knowledge obtained through meditation. German philosopher Olenberg suggests that the meaning of Upanishad signifies 'Upasana', bringing about oneness with the object worshipped or meditated. His meaning is not different from others who have explained in the similar fashion. It appears his meaning is closer to the *Rig Veda*, 'approaching respectfully with praise.'

The Upanishads vary greatly in numbers. In his book, *History of Indian Literature*, published in 1852, A. Weber referred from 108 to 235, Dara Shikoh translated 50 Upanishads, Paul Deussen translated and commented on 16, and 14 of them are originals. English author A.B. Keith translated 14 Upanishads. Shankaracharya recognised 16 Upanishads and commented on 10 extensively, and included quotations from six other Upanishads in his commentary on *Brahma Sutra*.

The reason for this variation in the numbers of the Upanishads is that they have been quoted by different names that make the number higher. When the same Upanishad contains the same story told almost in the same words, they are not copied from one to another, but settled independently in a different locality by different teachers for different purposes. Shankaracharya's texts belong to one locality only, and different readings may have existed in other parts of India.

The following are the important and principal Upanishads:

1. *Brihadaranyaka*
2. *Kaushistaki*
3. *Aitareya*
4. *Katha*
5. *Chandogya*
6. *Maitrayana*
7. *Shvetashvatara*
8. *Manduya*
9. *Mundaka*
10. *Prashna*
11. *Kena*
12. *Kaivala*
13. *Taittiriya*
14. *Isha*

Nirguna and Saguna Brahman

Paul Deussen in his book, *Element of Metaphysics*, brilliantly explains the theory of the great Indian philosopher, Shankaracharya, of 'Saguna and Nirguna Brahman' with the support of metaphysics. In fact, it is the summary of the whole philosophy of the Upanishads to a remarkable degree of success for the understanding of the common man.

He says, to know the nature of things is to separate the imperishable from the temporal. It can be done in two ways, through physics and transcendental methods. Things we regard in form or shape, which they appear to human consciousness, are the results of physics and embrace all the physical sciences. Things that we try to discover, what things are in themselves, independent of human consciousness, are the results of transcendental. Transcendental method proceeds from the fact that the sum total of our experience is things in themselves. The representation of things is built up out of these two methods which we call experience. All our knowledge begins with perception, which is partly internal and partly external.

All that we know and learn by the study of nature are called phenomenon in space and time linked together with the chain of causality. The cause and effect is called the law of causality. Every change in matter is called effect, and takes place only after another change called cause. A change from cause to effect is certain and cannot be disputed, but a change from effect to cause is problematical. The quality of every natural phenomenon is that it manifests an inner unity called force or energy.

Shankaracharya argues that Saguna Brahman (shape or form) can be achieved through worship. In contrast is Nirguna (Brahman), according to the *Brihadaranyaka Upanishads,* which says that whatever attempt you make to know Atman, whatever description you give him is *neti, neti* (It is not so. It is not so). When Vaskali asked Rishi Bharva to explain Brahman, he kept silent. King Vaskali repeated his request again and again. The rishi finally answered, "I tell it you, but you do not understand. This Atman is silence." Kant has also demonstrated that spaceless and timeless are not objective realities but only subjective forms of our intellect and extended in space, time and causality, being merely a representation of the mind and nothing beyond it. In Kantian philosophy Rishi Bharva is correct as the very constitution of our intellect excludes us from the knowledge of spaceless and timeless, godly realities forever. Yet the Atman is not unattainable to us, is not even far from us. We have it fully and totally in us.

For Shankaracharya, the world is illusion and *maya* and Plato expresses the same view—that the world is of shadows, not the things in it. It is appearance only.

Jiva (man) cannot be part of Brahman (God) because Brahman is without parts and all parts are either succession in time or coordinate in space. We are not different from Brahman.

The essence of all this is that *jiva,* being neither a part, nor different, nor a variation, must be Paramatman, fully and totally himself. Shankara further says, "If our soul is not a part of Brahman but Brahman itself, then all the attributes of Brahman, space, time, etc. are ours. 'I am Brahman.' Consequently, I am all pervading, spaceless and timeless." But these Godly qualities are hidden in us, just as the fire is hidden in the wood, butter in the milk, which will appear in the final deliverance.

What is the cause of this concealment of these Godly qualities?

The five *indrias*, *prana* and *karma* accompany Atman in migration without affecting its Godly nature, as the crystal is not infected by the colour painted over it. But whenever they originate, they are part of *maya* and based on our ignorance. We make mistakes all the time, that this world is real. We can compare a snake with a rope or a dream. A man whilst dreaming does not doubt the reality of the dream, but this reality vanishes at the moment of awakening to give place to a reality which he was not aware of whilst dreaming. Similarly, Brahman is hidden within us like a dream. Therefore, we are in ignorance to take the world as reality.

What is the cause of this ignorance or *maya*?

Shankara says the fundamental characteristic of this *avidya* or ignorance is that we are here in ignorance, sin and misery. It has no cause. The causality goes only as far as this world of *karma* and connecting each link with another, but never beyond.

The knowledge of this Atman, *aham brahma asi*, does not produce liberation but is liberation itself. You shall love your neighbour as yourselves because you are your neighbour and mere illusion makes you believe that your neighbour is different from you. The *Gita* also repeats it—who knows himself will not injure himself by himself. This is the total morality and this is the standpoint of a man knowing himself as Brahman. He feels himself as everything, so he will not desire anything. He lives in this world surrounded by illusion but not deceived by it. Therefore, he knows that there is only one Brahman, the Atman, his own Self, and verifies it by his own deeds of pure disinterested morality. And when death comes, he enters into Brahman like streams into ocean. He leaves behind his name and *rupa*, but does not leave Atman. It is not a fall of a drop in the ocean but is the whole ocean.

Kena Upanishad

Kena Upanishad belongs to *Sama Veda,* and has two parts. The first part is in a metrical poetry, and the second part is in prose, dealing with the relationship between gods and Brahman.

Brahman cannot be explained in words but by which the tongue speaks. The mind cannot be comprehended but by which the mind comprehends. The eyes do not see it but by which the eyes see. It is not drawn by breath but which draws the breath. If you think you are not Brahman, you know nothing. What is indeed the truth of Brahman that you must learn?

It is ignorant to think that Brahman is known, and wise to think that Brahman is beyond knowledge. One who realises that the existence of Brahman in every activity of his being like sensing, perceiving or thinking, he alone gains immortality. Brahman is the Self in all beings.

There is a legend in the Vedas that has been described in this Upanishad—about the nature of relationship between gods and Brahman. Once the *devas* defeated the demons in the battlefield and boasted that they had defeated them by their might and valour. Brahman saw the vanity of the gods, and appeared before them in the form of spirit.

The other gods said to the fire god, "Go and find out who this mysterious spirit is."

"Yes," the fire god said, and approached the spirit

The spirit said to him, "Who are you?"

"I am the god of fire and famous throughout the universe. I can burn anything on earth."

The spirit placed a straw before him and said, "Burn this."

The fire god fell upon it and failed to consume it. He ran back to the wind god and said, "I cannot discover who this mysterious spirit is."

This time the wind god went to discover the identity of the spirit. The wind god approached him. The spirit asked the wind god, "Who are you?"

"I am the god of wind and well known in the entire universe. I can blow away anything on earth."

The spirit placed a straw before him, "Blow this away."

The wind god fell upon it and failed to move it. He went back and said to the other gods, "I am unable to discover who this mysterious spirit is."

Later all other gods assembled and approached the king of gods, Indra, and requested him to find out the identity of the spirit.

Indra went to the spirit, but the spirit disappeared, and in his place Goddess Uma stood. Indra asked her, "Mother, who was the spirit that appeared to us?"

Uma answered, "That was Brahman. You attained victory and glory because of him, not by yourselves." Now all the gods recognised Brahman.

This truth of Brahman in relation to nature gods, in relation to man, in the motions of the wind, is the power shown in the universe, the power of Brahman. For this reason one should meditate upon Brahman and not worldly objects, as they are the source of illusion and ignorance.

One should learn, acquire and realise the knowledge of Brahman in meditation. This is the secret of knowledge. For this, one should prepare oneself for austerity, self-control, duty, etc. These are the bodies and arms of that knowledge. The Vedas are limbs. Truth is its soul.

Katha Upanishad

The *Katha Upanishad* belongs to the *Yajur Veda,* and consists of 120 stanzas divided into two sections. It is most remarkable and the most beautiful of the Upanishad*s*. The first chapter deals with the nature of Atman. In the second chapter the system of yoga is taught by means of obtaining the highest goal. There is a legend in the first chapter of King Vajasrabasa and his son Nachiketa that has been told in the *Taittiriya Brahmana*.

Once King Vajasrabasa performed the rite to seek divine favour. In the sacrifice the king was supposed to give away all his costly possessions. Instead he gave away the useless cows and barren land. Observing this, his son Nachiketa thought, that surely such a worshipper is doomed to utter darkness. He came to his father and said, "Offer me to the king of death as these worthless possessions will not bring divine favour to you." After repeated requests by his son, the king agreed to offer him in sacrifice.

Nachiketa travelled to the house of Yama who was not at home, and waited for three nights in the guest-house. After three days Yama returned home and was told by his servants that a brahmin boy was waiting for him since three days, in the guest-house. Hearing this Yama went to the guest-house and welcomed the brahmin boy with the words, "You waited three days at my guest-house without any hospitality. You may ask three boons for three nights."

The first wish was that when he returned to earth his father recognise and welcome him.

"Granted," the Yama replied.

The second wish was to teach the fire sacrifice. Yama taught him to conduct the fire ceremony. The boy learnt it by heart. The king of death became very pleased and declared, "Henceforth this sacrifice is called Nachiketa sacrifice."

For the third wish young Nachiketa chose the answer to the question, whether man exists after death or not. "I would like to know the truth."

Nirguna and Saguna Brahman

Yama replied, "Even the gods were once puzzled by this mystery. It is not easy to understand. Choose another wish. I will offer you cattle, elephants, gold and all the riches of this world for another wish."

Nachiketa stood fast and said, "These things only last till tomorrow. I know the vanity of the flesh as they are subject to decay and death. How can I choose another wish?"

Yama was pleased at heart and began to teach the secret of immortality. He said, "Life and death are different phases of development. True knowledge is the possession beyond the realm of death.

"Meditate on *Aum*. It is the symbol and syllable of the Self. He is neither born nor dies. He is neither cause nor effect.

"He is eternal though the body is destroyed. He is not destroyed. This syllable *Aum* is the Brahman and Supreme.

"Know that Self is the rider, and body is the chariot, intellect is the charioteer and mind is the reins. The senses are horses; the roads they travel are on the mazes of desire.

"When man has discrimination and his mind is controlled, his senses obey the reins. As pure water poured into pure water remains pure, so does the Self remain pure, uniting this with Brahman.

"The mind is higher than the senses. The intellect is higher than the mind. The ego is higher than the intellect. The unmanifested seed is higher than the ego, the primal cause.

"When the senses are stilled, the mind is at rest, the intellect does not shake, then man reaches to the highest state.

"This calm of the senses, and the mind has been defined as Yoga. He who attains it is freed from delusion."

Thus, Nachiketa learned this knowledge and the whole process of Yoga. He was freed from impurities and from death, and was united with Brahman.

Chandogya Upanishad

This a very old, remarkable and widely quoted Upanishad by ancient and modern philosophers. It is written in prose and belongs to *Sama Veda*. The fundamental doctrine of the Upanishad is the identity of the individual Self expressed most forcefully in the *Chandogya*. An old story has been mentioned in it that was popular in the Upanishad age amongst the population. The story is about man who learnt and realised the Self, free from impurities, from death, from illness, from grief and such a man obtained both the worlds (heaven and earth) and all his desires were fulfilled. That is real, that is soul, THAT ART THOU.

Once all the gods and demons decided to send their king, Indra, and King Virochana of the demons to Prajapati to learn about the Self. Both went to Prajapati and lived with him for 32 years as disciples. After these long years Prajapati asked them why they both had lived for such a long time with him. They replied that they had heard a story, one who realised the Self obtained both worlds and all his desires were fulfilled. "We lived here, as we would learn about Self."

Both enquired, "Sir, the Self is that which is reflected to be seen in still water."

Prajapati replied, "Look at yourselves in the water and tell me about it."

Both of them looked carefully at their reflections in the water, returned and said to the Prajapati, "We have seen the Self, even the nails and ears."

Now Prajapati gave them new and beautiful clothes to wear and asked them to look again in the water. They looked again in the water at their beautiful clothes and said to Prajapati, "We have seen the Self, it is very handsome in these beautiful clothes." Prajapati replied, "The Self is indeed seen in beautiful clothes, the Self is fearless, the Self is Brahman."

Hearing this Indra and Virochana were very pleased and departed with the teacher to their homes without discriminating and analysing the statement of the teacher. Virochana returned to the demons and began to teach other demons that the body should be worshipped as well as served, and one who worships the body gains both worlds and all one's desires are fulfilled.

Since then it has become the fundamental doctrine of the demons to worship the body to conquer the worlds.

On the way back Indra realised that this knowledge of the Self was useless. If the body was sick, the Self would be sick, and when the body died so the Self would die. Indra came back to Prajapati and lived with him for another 64 years and gained the knowledge that was useless to the understanding of the real Self. Once more he returned to Prajapati who made him stay for another five years. When five years passed Prajapati taught him the true knowledge of the Self.

He instructed, "This body is perishable and always surrounded by death and danger, but within it lives the immortal Self. When the Self is attached and associated with the body it is subject to pain and pleasure, happiness and unhappiness, sorrow and grief. One cannot get freedom as long as this attachment and association of the body and Self exists. When the body is dissociated and detached, it is the end of pain and pleasure." In other words, "rising above the physical consciousness." The knowledge of the Self is separate from the senses and the mind. One who knows this truth becomes free.

Since then it has become the doctrine of the gods to "rise above the senses and mind" for the true knowledge of the Self. The association of the body with the Self should be ceased.

Once Uddalaka said to his son, Svetaketu, "You are twelve years old and go to school and study. None of our family members is ignorant of Brahman." He went to school and learnt all the sciences, music, philosophy, art and read scriptures. When he returned home after his education, his father asked him, "Do you know about Brahman?"

Svetaketu replied, "What is that knowledge, sir?"

"My child, as by knowing a lump of clay, all things made of clay are known, the difference is only in the name arising out of speech. The truth being that all are clay, exactly so is with the Self."

In the beginning there was One existence, One only without a second, and out of that the universe was born. He, the One, thought, Let me be many, let me grow forth. Thus out of Himself He projected the universe and entered into being.

Of all things He is the subtle essence. He is the truth. He is the Self; THAT ART THOU.

"Bees make honey by collecting juices from many flowers of different trees and plants, and reduce them to one honey. They do not know from what flowers it comes." In the same way creatures like the lion, bear, monkey know nothing of this past. All these creatures—when they merge in that one existence – know not that they are merged in Him and that from Him they come.

"Please, sir, tell me more about this Self," the son requested his father.

"Bring me a fruit of the tree."

"Here it is, sir."

"Break it."

"It is broken, sir."

"What do you see?"

"Some seeds, extremely small."

"Break one of them."

"It is broken, sir."

"What do you see?

"Nothing, sir,"

"The subtle essence you do not see, and in that is the whole tree. That is the truth. That is the Self; THAT ART THOU."

"Please tell me some more about the Self."

"Put this salt in the water, and come to me tomorrow morning."

Svetaketu put the salt in the water. The next morning his father asked him to bring the salt, which he had put in the water the previous day. He failed to bring the salt as it had dissolved. Then his father said to him,

"Taste this water, and tell me how it tastes."

"It is salty, sir.

The father continued, "You do not see Brahman in this body, He is indeed here in the body. Like salt has dissolved in the water, so the Brahman has dissolved in the body. That is that subtle essence – in that we have our existence. That is the truth. That is the Self."

Once Narada came to Sanatkumar and requested him to accept him as a pupil.

Sanatkumar asked him, "What have you learned already?"

Narada replied that he had studied all the branches of learning, art, science, philosophy and music, and read the scriptures. "Still I am not at peace; my mind is always worried, as I do not know the Self. I have heard from teachers that he who knows the Self overcomes grief."

Sanatkumar said, "Whatever you have read is only names. Meditate on names as Brahman."

Narada asked, "Is there anything higher than name?"

"Yes, speech is higher than name. It is through speech we come to know what is right or wrong, what is true or false. If there is no speech neither truth nor falsehood would be known.

Meditate on speech as Brahman."

"Sir, is there anything higher than speech?"

"Yes, mind is higher than speech. It is the mind that holds the name and speech. The mind is the inner organ of the Self. It is the means of happiness. Meditate on the mind as Brahman."

"Sir, is there anything higher than the mind?"

"Yes, will is higher than the mind. Name, speech and mind, all these centres are in the will. Meditate on the will as Brahman."

"Sir, is there anything higher than the will?"

"Yes, discriminating will is higher than the will. Meditate on discriminating will as Brahman."

"Sir, is there anything higher than the discriminating will?"

"Yes, concentration is higher than the discriminating will. Men achieve greatness on earth through concentration. Mean and shallow people are always quarrelling and fighting for lack of concentration. Great men who concentrate always get their reward. Meditate on concentration as Brahman."

"Sir, is there anything higher than concentration?"

"Yes, insight is higher than concentration. It is through insight that we understand right and wrong, the true and false. Meditate on insight as Brahman."

Lastly, Sanatkumar taught Narada to meditate on Brahman as power, as food, as principles of life.

"Sir, I wish to be a true knower."

"One who respects one's teacher, gains faith and reverence that reflect eternal truth."

"Sir, what is joy, I want to know?"

" The Infinite is the source of joy. There is no joy in the finite."

"Sir, what is the Infinite?"

"Where one sees nothing but One, hears nothing but One, knows nothing but One. Where one sees the other or many is finite. The Infinite is immortal and the finite is mortal and perishable.

"The Infinite rests in Its own glory. It rests in Itself. He becomes master of Himself. Slaves are they who do not know the truth. The whole universe issues forth from it."

Brihadaranyaka Upanishad

It is one of the oldest, longest and most important Upanishads. It has also been most referred, quoted and commented upon by most of the scholars and religious leaders. It belongs to *Yajur Veda* and deals with the origin of creation, knowledge of the Self and Brahman. At the beginning Atman and Brahman was the universe, and in its loneliness, felt no pleasure. Desiring a second being, He became man and woman whence the human race was produced. Then proceeded male and female, and finally creating water, air, fire and so forth. Whosoever knows this 'I am Brahman' becomes all. Even gods are not able to prevent him from becoming It. He becomes their Self (Atman). This Brahman is without cause, without effect, without inside or outside. This Brahman is the Self.

The ear, breath, speech and thought are all names, forms and acts. One who worships these does not understand the Self. Knowing the Self one knows all. This universe existed as Brahman before creation. Anyone who knows and understands that these are different from the Self does not understand Brahman.

One day, Gargya, son of Vakala, went to the king of Benaras, Ajatashatru, and said that he would teach him about Brahman. He began to tell that the spirit in the sun, in the air, in the sound, in the mind are Brahman, and "I meditate on him as Brahman." After hearing this, the king said to him, "That is all you know. In fact you do not know Brahman." Gargya requested the king,

"Please accept me as a disciple." Ajatashatru was surprised that a brahmin came to a kshatriya to learn about Brahman. One day, as both were walking on the road, they saw a man sleeping. Ajatashatru said to the sleeping man, "Sire." The man did not reply. But when he touched his body he woke up. Now Ajatashatru pointed to Gargya, "In the sleeping state he knows nothing and enters in the Self. He might be dreaming that he is a king, emperor or angel, etc. In deep sleep he has withdrawn into himself both his senses and his mind. He is supposed to be absorbed in the Self. In this state he knows nothing and finds rest. He lives in a world of his own. Just as a thread comes out of the spider, as a little spark comes out of the fire, so all the senses, all the worlds of the dream come out from the Self."

Once Yagnavalkya said to his wife, "Maitreyi, I want to renounce the world and wish to divide my wealth between you and my other wife."

"Will I attain immortality through wealth?" Maitreyi asked her husband.

"No one should hope to attain immortality through wealth," the king replied.

"Teach me the way of immortality," Maitreyi said to her husband.

"The Self, Maitreyi, is to be known. Hear about it, reflect upon it, meditate upon it. By knowing the Self one comes to know all things.

"The river, the mountain, the king, the priest, the creatures, etc., these are the Self. When the drum is beaten, its different notes are not heard apart from the whole, but in the total sound all its notes are heard. When the veena is played its different notes are not heard apart from the whole, but in the total sound all its notes are heard. So through the knowledge of the Self, all things and beings are known. There is no existence apart from the Self.

"Water is the centre of the ocean; touch is the centre of the skin; smell is the centre of the nose; and taste is the centre of the tongue.

"Form and sight are the centre of the eye; sound is the centre of the ears; thought is the centre of the mind; love is the centre of the heart; so for all beings are the one centre of the Self.

"As a lump of salt thrown into the water would dissolve and cannot be taken out again, the water, wherever tasted would be salty. The individual Self is dissolved in the Eternal, Infinite and Transcendental. Individuality arises by identification of the Self through ignorance. Where there is consciousness of the Self, individuality is no more.

"As long as there is duality, one sees the other, one hears the other, one smells the other, and one speaks the other. But when the other melts away in the Self, who is there to be seen, heard, spoken to by whom? The Self is described, as not this, not that. It is incomprehensible, undecaying, unattached and unbound. By who shall be known?

"The Self is the Lord of all beings, King of all beings. As spokes are held together in the hub and in the felly of a wheel, so all beings and all creatures are held together in the Self. He assumed all forms to reveal Himself in all forms. He is revealed in all forms through his *maya* and illusion."

On one occasion the king of Videha, Janaka, performed a sacrifice and distributed costly gifts. In the assembly wise men of Kuru and Panchala were also present. King Janaka addressed the assembly, "Respected Brahmins, whosoever is the wisest in the assembly may take away thousand cows with ten gold coins fastened between the horns."

Yagnavalkya was among the audience and said to his disciples, "Drive away my cows." The disciples cried in joy. The brahmins who were present in the assembly were enraged, "How dare he call himself the wisest in the assembly!" they shouted.

At last, Aswala, the chief priest of King Janaka, addressed, "Are you quite sure you are the wisest?"

He then asked Yagnavalkya, "As everything of the sacrifice is pervaded by death and subject to death, by what means can a worshipper overcome death?"

Yagnavalkya answered, "By the knowledge of the worshipper, fire and *mantra* of the sacrifice. This knowledge leads one beyond death."

On another occasion, Janaka, having seated himself to give audience, saw sage Yagnavalkya among his visitors and addressed him.

"What brings you here? Do you come here for cattle or philosophy?"

"For both."

King Janaka requested the sage, "Teach me the knowledge of the Self."

"The Self, having in the dreams enjoyed the pleasures of senses, gone here and there, experienced good and evil, fear and courage, hastens back to the state of waking from which he started. As man passes from one dream to wakefulness, so does he pass at death from one life to the next. As a leech, having reached the end of a blade of grass, takes hold of another blade of grass and draws itself to it, so the Self, having left this body behind, draws Himself to it unconsciously, takes the form of another *jiva* and draws Himself to it. As a goldsmith, taking the old gold ornament, moulds it into another, newer and more beautiful, so the Self, have given up the *jiva* and left it unconsciously, takes a new and better form.

"This Self is Brahman. A man through *maya* or ignorance identifies himself with what is alien to him. As a man acts, so does he become. A man of good deeds becomes good, by evil deeds become evil. By the purified mind alone Brahman is perceived. In Brahman there is no duality. He who sees diversity goes from one death to another death.

"Brahman can be apprehended only as knowledge itself, knowledge that is one with reality, inseparable from it. It is beyond all proof. The eternal Brahman is unborn, undying, and universal; fearlessness is the very truth of Brahman."

Shvetashvatara Upanishad

The central doctrine of this Upanishad is, what is the cause of the universe?

Time, space, matter, energy, intelligence, etc., none of these, or a combination of these, can be a final cause of the universe, for they are effects, and exist to serve the soul.

The seers saw within themselves the ultimate reality of one God. He presides over time, space and all apparent causes.

This vast universe is a wheel upon which all creatures exist, being subject to birth, death and rebirth. It is the wheel of Brahman. As long as the individual himself thinks, it is separate from Brahman, it revolves upon the wheel in the bondage to the laws of birth and death. But when an individual realises its identity within him, it does not revolve around the wheel any longer. He achieves immortality. As soon as an individual transcends the world of cause and effect, he is imperishable and becomes Brahman.

Like oil in the sesame seeds, butter in the cream, water in the riverbed, fire in the tinder, the Self dwells within the soul. Realise Him through meditation.

As a soiled piece of metal, when cleaned, shines brightly, so the Dweller in the body. When he has realised the truth of the Self he loses he his sorrow and becomes radiant with bliss.

He moves fast, though without feet. He grasps everything, though without hands. He sees everything, though without eyes, He hears everything, though without ears. He knows all that is, but no one knows Him. He is called the Supreme. He is subtler than the subtlest, greater than the greatest. The Self is hidden in the heart of all creatures.

Mundaka, Prashna, Maitrayana & Manduka Upanishads

The *Mundaka, Prashna* and *Manduka* are the most important Upanishads of *Atharva Veda*, and the first two are original. The *Mundaka* borrows its name from the monks who shaved their heads. It is most popular owing to the purity with which it reproduces old doctrines of the Vedanta. It deals with the preparations for the knowledge of Brahman, the doctrine of Brahman and the way to Brahman.

The sage must distinguish between knowledge and wisdom. Knowledge is of the things, acts and relations. But wisdom is Brahman alone and beyond all things, acts and relations. He abides forever. To become one with Him is the only wisdom.

The *Prashna Upanishad* is written in prose and deals with the main points of the Vedanta philosophy. It describes the origin of matter and life. It explains that breath or *prana* is born of the Self like a man and his shadow. The Self and *prana* are inseparable. *Prana* enters the body at birth, desires the mind, continuing from the past lives, and may be fulfilled.

The *Manduka* is a very short Upanishad, which hardly covers two pages of this book. The fundamental characteristic of this Upanishad is that the syllable *Aum* is an expression of the universe and Brahman and one can meditate upon this syllable.

The *Maitrayana Upanishad* is written in prose and belongs to the *Yajur Veda*. It consists of seven chapters devoted to the Sankhya System. It has described three qualities of matter: *Tamas, Rajas* and *Sattva*, connected with Rudra, Vishnu and Shiva. As a means of attaining Brahman, it has prescribed the practice of Yoga leading to mental concentration.

Sutras

Sutra is a Sanskrit word that means 'thread' or 'clue' in English to discover the information from the massive literature of the Vedas and Brahmanas. Vedic scholars are unable to assign any date like other literature of origin when they were first composed. The source of Sutras can be searched back into the Vedas and Brahmanas as they deal with the matters compiled in the Vedic literature. Sutras are brief and short compendious treatises dealing with rituals on the one hand, and customary law on the other. The rise of this class of literature was due to the needs of reducing the vast growing massive details in the ritual custom. The main purpose is to provide a short and brief glimpse of the sum of these scattered details laid out in the Vedas and Brahmanas. These Sutras are not concerned with the interpretation or explanation of ceremonies or traditions, but aim to provide a plain and methodical account of the whole course of ritual practices observed in an Aryan family. These Sutras are compiled in a mixed form of poetry and prose, like the Upanishads, and compressed to the level of the algebraic mode.

These Sutras are so concise that they cannot be understood without commentaries of the experts in the field as they are handed down from one generation to another. The tradition was handed down into two forms. One class of Sutras was based on *sruti* or revelation or hearing. The *Sruti Sutras* deal with the rituals of greater sacrifices observed by a village, town, and country or by a king in the country joined by thousands of people. In such sacrifices several priests as well as several *havan kundas* are required. The second form of ritual Sutras are called *Grihya Sutras* based on *smriti* or tradition, and related with the household ceremonies by a domestic fire. The householder, wife and children perform these rites.

The second class of Sutras is concerned with social and legal matters based on tradition or *smriti*. These are also called *Dharma Sutras* or *Dharma Shastras*. They are very closely connected with the Vedas, the highest source of *Dharma*. The *Dharma Sutras* are of great significance to the religious institutions. They have further value in the life of an Aryan as he is surrounded by a network of religious practices in daily life, from birth to death, even after death in the family. From the literary point of view they are not as good as the Brahmanas but have great importance as regards contents. Different Vedic schools composed these Sutras as every Veda and *Brahmana* has its own Sutra. A famous law book of Gautama (not Buddha) is well preserved connected with Vedic school of *Sama Veda*. Another, called *Dharma Shastra* of Vasishtha belonging to the Vedic school, is preserved and studied by the disciples of the *Rig Veda* only.

These *Grihya Sutras* give rules to practise numerous ceremonies applicable to the domestic life of an Aryan and his family. There are about 40 ceremonies in the life of a Hindu male member and only one of a female member. Eighteen of them are performed from conception to marriage. The first ceremony is a wish to obtain a son. The second is the naming ceremony after birth; another is the *mundan* (tonsure) ceremony at the age of three. The most important ceremony before marriage is called *upanayana* (initiation) and it can take place at any age from eight to 16. Another most important ceremony is the marriage when the bride and bridegroom take seven steps around the fire and take a bow to live together till death. It is only one ceremony of the female member of the family. One ceremony is of funeral. All the members of the family should be cremated and their ashes should be scattered in a holy river of flowing water. A child under the age of two who dies should be buried and not cremated. These ceremonies and rites play an important part in the life of an Aryan even today. Some ceremonies are performed as duties of a householder, i.e., to recite and study the Vedas for the purification of the mind and heart. Very few sacrifices occur periodically like building a new house, moving the house, agriculture, trade or achieving success in ventures of any type. There are some to avoid unseen calamity.

The *Dharma Sutras* are based on *sruti* or traditions, composed at the beginning of the *Sutra* period. There are others that are concerned duties of a householder of an Aryan family like forbidden food, purification, penance, law of marriage, inheritance, crime, etc.

Upa-sutras or Supplementary Sutras

In the *Sutra* age another work of great importance arose to protect the Vedic literature, called auxiliary or *Upa-sutras*. They are not religious and do not deal with religious matters at all in any capacity. They arose from the study of the Vedas and Brahmanas. These Sutras are called *Pratichakhya Sutras* and deal with the accentuation of *mantras,* pronunciation, metre of the poetry and other matters concerning phonetics and grammar. The correct and exact pronunciation and methodical procedure (*vidhi*) of the *havans* and ceremonies are necessary for the desired results. The chief object is to ensure the correct recitation and interpretation of the sacred texts and *mantras*. The origin of these is religious but the end is not so.

There are four treatises of *Pratichakhya* or *Upa-sutras* which have been preserved, and some of them are lost or damaged.

One supplementary Sutra is connected with the *Rig Veda*, another with the *Atharva Veda*. Two are connected with the *Yajur*, which are called by the name of *Vajasaneyi* and *Taittiriya Samhita*.

Yet in the *Sutra* period another work of great significance also emerged to protect the Vedic literature from loss, damage or change in the future. Their aim was to preserve the Vedas intact by registering its contents from various points of views. Their style is unintelligible in nature, hard to understand by a novice or beginner, and inferior to the literary productions of the previous and earlier Vedic productions. They are called *Anukramanis* or indices. These indices give the first word of every hymn, the name of the author, the gods who are celebrated, and the metre in which hymns are composed. One of the indices even supply the total number of verses of hymns and even syllables contained in the *Vedas* and other details as well. In brief, they are like the index of a book or bibliography.

Puranas (Sanskrit Literature)

The third religion of the Vedic literature begins in a formal fashion from the Sutras and continues to date. During the *Sutra* phase the trinity of gods—Indra, Vishnu and Shiva—appeared, and in the Puranic era some new gods like Ganesh, Parvati, Kubera, Durga and other goddesses came into prominence. For the first time temples were built to worship these gods in the Aryan land. In Vedic literature these gods are not mentioned and it is assumed that nature gods of the Vedas occupied a secondary place of worship. Rather, it can be said that they were assimilated and became a part of the temple worship for the domestic life of a householder. It was possibly intended to reach devotion to children, women and the unlearned class of the land, who were unable to comprehend the abstract gods of the Upanishads and devotion to the nature gods. It has made the religion and worship reach every individual of the society. Sutras prepared the groundwork for the worship of images and idols to be easily accessible to the entire population of the land.

The word 'Purana' is a Sanskrit word, meaning very old or ancient in English. The word 'Purana' is found in the Brahmanas and Vedas of old collection of legends, relating stories about gods. Some of the materials and contents of the Puranas are common with the great epic, *Mahabharata*. The object of these legendary compilations is to advocate the worship of Vishnu and Shiva. In its approach the Puranas are connected with the old law books and Vedas, representing a development of older works of the same class. These Puranas were written in poetry as well as in prose.

There are 18 Puranas in total. Half of the Puranas deal with and describe three things in general. Firstly, they describe stories of gods and genealogies of the sages, saints, kings, heroes and warriors. Secondly, they deal with mystical descriptions of the earth, doctrines of the cosmic ages and accounts of the *avatars* of Vishnu and Shiva. Thirdly, they contain rules about the worship of temple gods by means of prayers, fasting, offerings, festivals, pilgrimage, etc. The rest half of the Puranas describe and explain the cosmogony of the Sankhya system. One will find that the purity of Sankhya ideas and themes of Puranic Sankhya is a concept of *Purusha* (spirit) as male and *Prakrit* (matter) as a female principle of creation. It is said that Urasravas, the son of a rishi, related the contents of Sankhya on the occasion of a sacrifice in a Namisha forest. The important Puranas that describe the worship of Vishnu and Shiva are *Bhagavata, Vishnu, Markandeya, Matsya, Vayu, Padma, Shiva, Skanda, Bhavishyat Puranas*, etc.

The *Bhagavata Purana* contains 18,000 *shlokas* and it derived its name from being dedicated to the glorification of Vishnu. It commands the most powerful influence in the whole of India when compared with the other Puranas. The most popular section is the tenth book, which describes the history of Lord Krishna in great depth and detail.

The *Vayu Purana* is accepted as the oldest, and it describes the creation of the world. It explains that the world is represented by having several islands separated by different oceans. The central island is a Jambu-dvipa and Aryavarta; the kingdom of Bharat is the main division.

The *Padma Purana* explains the trinity of the gods—Brahma, Vishnu and Shiva. In conclusion it comes to explain that these three are only One and not the three in the form of preserver, destroyer and creator. This *Purana* also describes the story of Rama, the son of Dasharatha. Besides the trinity it deals with the story of Shakuntala and Raghuvansha, that have become world-famous plays of Kalidasa. It also relates the story of Radha and Krishna.

The *Vishnu Purana* explains five topics of primary and secondary creation, and the history of the old dynasties of the kings of Aryavarta. The chronology mentions Surayavanshi kings and the thousand names of Vishnu and Shiva.

The *Markandeya Purana* is connected with Rishi Markandeya and describes the birth of Lord Krishna in the form of a man who is a part of the *Mahabharata* epic.

The *Matsya Purana* is related with the story of Brahman in the form of a fish, and explains how the fish flowed in a flood and was saved by a sage. That is the cause of creation.

The three Puranas—*Skanda, Shiva* and *Bhavishyat*—recommend the worship of Shiva. These Puranas are ritualistic in nature rather than worshipful.

Besides these 18 Puranas, there are an equal number of *Upa-puranas* or secondary Puranas. The secondary Puranas are also ritualistic in nature, and do not describe the worship, creation or cosmic age. Some of these supplementary Puranas did not survive and were lost in transition. All these Puranas are didactic in character, and intended to instruct or teach the reader or worshipper to follow the rules of worship and learn the ancient history of Vedic and pre-Vedic age.

Mahabharata

Mahabharata is recognised as an encyclopaedia of moral behaviour and characterised in terms of Dharma Shastra.

Sanskrit literature falls under two main categories: legend and narrative. The *Mahabharata* falls in the category of legends and the *Ramayana* in the narrative. Both these epics are composed in the *shloka* metre of two lines contrary to the Vedas composed in the stanzas of four lines. The *Mahabharata* may be distinguished from the *Ramayana* in that it contains speeches, which do not form part of the poetry. The seeds of these epics are pre-Vedic and mentioned in the Vedas and Brahmanas.

The story of *Mahabharata* supports the pre-Vedic conflict between the two neighbouring tribes of Panchalas and Kurus. The Panchala Pradesh covers the territory from Meerut to Benaras and Kuru Pradesh from Haryana to Rajasthan including Delhi. In the *Yajur Veda* both tribes were united into a single tribe, and King Vaichi Travirya appeared to be a respectable and famous king in the land of Aryavarta. The conflict of both the tribes reappeared in the story of *Mahabharata*. The conflict between the two tribes subsided by artificial unity for several generations, and reappeared in the form of the famous war between the close cousins. We also find the names of Bharat and *Mahabharata* in the *Grihya Sutra* as well. The legend is not an independent creation, but the germs of the two opposing clans are earlier than the Vedas. Therefore, a historical background of the epic was planted in the Vedas itself and compiled by Vyasa, the son of Rishi Parasar.

The epic *Mahabharata* contains more than one lakh *shlokas* of two lines in addition to several speeches equal to eight times as much as the *Iliad* and *Odyssey* put together, and the longest poem known to any literature of the past and present. The *Mahabharata* is divided into 18 books and a supplementary book called the nineteenth book. These 18 books vary in length, and the twelfth is the largest, consisting of 14,000 *shlokas*. The seventeenth is the shortest, containing 312 *shlokas* only. Many of the modern editions of the epic ignore the supplementary book, and a few *shlokas* here and there for the purpose of better reading without harming the essence of the epic. Twenty thousand *shlokas* describe 18 days of battle between the cousins, Pandu and Kaurav.

It is a heroic poem of extraordinary valour, described in the battle. The epic was intended for moral teaching to all Aryans as well as non-Aryans. The epic represents four purposes of human existence on earth based on morality: merit, wealth, salvation and pleasure. The virtue of justice, truth and duty are preserved in the story.

The *Mahabharata* is an essence of the Vedas, Upanishad*s* and Sutras assimilated in the philosophy of the trinity of Bhakti, Knowledge and Karma Yoga.

The eighteenth chapter of the epic is a dialogue between lord Krishna and Arjuna about the duty of a warrior in a battlefield. It is called 'Krishna Veda' or fifth Veda.

Several episodes have been mentioned in the story of *Mahabharata* taken from the earlier Vedic literature such as

Shakuntala, the episode of the fish, Nala-Damayanti, Satyavan-Savitri, etc. All these episodes have been developed in the post-Sanskrit literature and are very famous in their own rights. We also find numerous miraculous and supernatural features in the epic that suggest the role of the divine hand on the side of righteousness, and victory in favour of *Dharma*. Therefore, the *Mahabharata* is recognised as an encyclopaedia in terms of *Dharma Shastra*.

The nineteenth book of the *Mahabharata* is called Harivansha or family of Vishnu connected with Lord Krishna. It contains 16,000 *shlokas* and divided into three sections or sub-books. The first section of the supplementary deals with the story of Krishna's ancestors down to the Vishnu incarnation of Krishna. The second section deals with the actions and activities of Krishna from birth to death. The third section describes about Kaliyuga or the fourth stage of the world.

Ramayana

Ramayana is a celestial myth transformed into a narrative terrestrial adventure (Jacobi).

Every Aryan is an offspring of the great monument and document of the excellent genius of the *Rig Veda* known to mankind and civilisation. The plant of *Rig Veda* arose on the soil itself, and rishis of the Vedas were the medium. We are its flowers, fruits and leaves that will spread to satisfy generations after generations to eternity. The foundations of the *Rig Veda* are so deep and strong that no hurricane can shake off its roots. The name of King Dasharatha and his son Rama have been mentioned in the *Rig*. Hence, the genius of the *Ramayana* is descended and adopted from the *Rig* near about Buddha's birth. In the opinion of the German philosopher, Jacobi, the *Ramayana* is based on Indian mythology adopted from the Vedas. It is a celestial myth transformed into a terrestrial adventure.

The character of Sita, the wife of Rama, can also be discovered in the *Rig* where she appears as a furrow personified and invoked as a goddess. In several *Grihya Sutras*, Sita again appeared as a genius of agriculture and was the wife of Indra, the rain god. We also find traces of this origin in the *Ramayana* itself. We also find that Sita was born from the earth when her father, King Janaka, was ploughing the field with the help of his employees, and disappeared in the arms of the earth. Rama is nothing else than Indra, the important god of the *Rig*. The demon Ravana also represents the myth of the *Rig*, the son of an enemy of Indra. The gods approached one of the gods of the trinity, Brahma, to be born again in the form of a human being. Vishnu was born as Rama to destroy demon king Ravana who had become most powerful by the kindness of Lord Shiva in a boon, and stole his wife Sita.

Ramayana does not contain very many episodes of divine interference in the form of supernatural or miraculous events like the *Mahabharata*. One of the divinities of the *Ramayana* brought down the sacred River Ganga from heaven to earth in order to purify the ashes of 60,000 sons of King Sagara, who were reduced to ashes when they disturbed the tapasya of Sage Kapila. Rishi Valmiki has also described another supernatural episode in the *Ramayana*.

One day, on the bank of river, a rishi was watching a pair of birds. A male bird was shot dead by a hunter. It fell on the ground, full of blood, before him. Valmiki was moved with grief to see the female who was restless due to the death of her partner, and planning to take a revenge of her partner on the wicked hunter. Lord Brahma appeared before him and ordered him to get on to compose the *shlokas* of the *Ramayana*, rather than feel sad over the death of the male bird. It was better to concentrate his mind and energy to conceive *shlokas* on the life and deeds of the great king Lord Rama. It appeared that the prophecy of Lord Brahma came true—that the *Ramayana* commands the greatest respect generations after generations in the whole of India.

The *Ramayana* contains 240,000 *shlokas* in seven books. Every householder of India, from Kanyakumari to Kashmir, keeps a copy of the *Ramayana* and recites with great emotions, joy and purity of spiritual feelings, as well as follows on the footsteps of Lord Rama as an ideal householder. Even India as a nation aspires to dream of Ram Rajya, so every citizen could lead his life happily.

The Valmiki *Ramayana* inspired the poet, Tulsidas, who composed the Sanskrit version into vernacular language, called *Tulsi Charitamanas*. The beauty and excellence of Tulsidas version is to keep alive the standard ideas of Vedic literature. It has become the Bible of millions of people in India. In every family of India several times the ideals of *Ramayana* are referred to in everyday life, as people like to lead their life on the ideals of Lord Rama.

Panchatantra

*Humans are part of animal nature and it should be
controlled by knowledge, not by doctrines.*

Vedic literature is holy and devotional, Sanskrit literature is religious and ethical. Fables are regarded as manuals of moral and intellectual instructions for teaching the right conduct through satire, amusement and quaint humour.

The last stage of Sanskrit literature is important, and valuable work has been done in the form of fables. The most significant book of fables is called the *Panchatantra*. 'Pancha' means five and 'Tantra' can be explained in terms of force, system, technique or method. It contains five books of satire and amusement. The word 'Tantra' comes from the Sanskrit root 'to weave', and refers to the interwovenness and interdependence of all things and events. The Buddhist literature used the words enormously and developed a separate system in its religion. Evidence also suggests that the word 'Tantra' has been used in Vedic literature in one form or another. At one stage, there were 12 books and the rest of them were damaged or lost in the interval of the original and Pehlavi translation of fifth century ad. From the literary point of view it is a valuable and interesting work in the branch of Indian literature. Mostly the importance of the fables has been neglected in India as it contains very little holiness and devotion. It is rather a manual of human behaviour and conduct. It has been written in prose, and to explain the story causally poetry has been included. In fact, it moulds the character and behaviour on the lines of right conduct.

The ancient literature of fables exerted an enormous influence and impact over the intellectual life of all the nations of the world. In the department of aphorism Indians have attained extraordinary excellence, which has never been acquired by any other nation on earth. The science of fables has become an independent branch of discipline on the famous work of *Panchatantra*. It is true that Buddha himself used fables to teach his disciples for the right conduct. It is impossible to say exactly when they were written like other Vedic literature. The Brahmanas and Upanishad*s* are the reservoir of legends and fables. It has been proved that rudimentary forms of fables were found in the *Chandogya Upanishad* and had risen at the time of Buddha. At the start of the Buddhist literature fables began to migrate throughout the whole world in ancient and middle ages. It may not be a Buddhist work but a large number of fables are found in Buddhist literature after the death of Buddha.

Fables came to the notice of the world when they were translated into Pehlavi language of Persia by the order of the King Khusrau in the fifth and sixth century AD. The two old Chinese encyclopaedias contain a large number of Indian fairy tales and fables translated into Chinese. About 200 fables were found in Chinese, translated from Buddhist literature as well.

The collection of fables is also found in *Hitopadesha* of very late and post-Sanskrit literature. This book of *Hitopadesha* is based on *Panchatantra,* and 25 out of 43 fables have been borrowed directly from the *Panchatantra* and the remaining 18 are original creation of its authors. Even today it is the most important book in India due to its intrinsic and in-built value of advice in the matter of human conduct.

These fables were translated from Pehlavi into Arabic in the sixth and seventh centuries AD, called *Kalilah* and *Dinnah*, by a converted Persian to Islam. The *Arabian Night* translation is also based on the *Panchatantra*. The Arabic translation is the most important source of other European translations. The first translation of the *Panchatantra* was made in AD 1180. The Spanish translation was carried out in AD 1251, and the Hebrew translation was conducted in AD 1250. The Latin translation was made from Hebrew in AD 1270. The most important translation from Latin to German was made in AD 1481 under the title *Book of Apologues of the Ancient Ages*. It was so popular and famous that four more editions were printed in AD 1483 and AD 1485, and 13 more editions were published in AD 1492. It shows the influence and importance of the *Panchatantra* as a means of right conduct through humour, satire and amusement during the later centuries. From the German translation the Italian version was published at Venice in AD 1562. From the Italian version Sir Thomas North made the English translation in AD 1570.

The popularity of the *Panchatantra* in the whole world is due to its unique character of stories. The characters of the stories are men and women, half men and half animals, birds, monkeys, tiger, wolf, cat, sparrow, parrots, etc. They talk about the follies of men and teach the rational nature of men and a code of ethics.

The French author of fairy tales and fables had paid great tributes and acknowledged his indebtedness of his work to Indians and particularly sage Vidyapati. This has been translated into Pilpay in Pehlavi. The French author preserved the story lines and changed the characters of the story in his famous work.

Originally, the *Panchatantra* was intended to be a catalogue of instructions to the children of kings and queens as well as the elite, in the principles of conduct in Indian society. These are pervaded by quaint humour to explain the morals, virtues and purity as well as vices. In them human vices are exposed in the conduct of human behaviour of government officials of the day and the character of the people. These vices have been explained in Indian fables more forcefully than anywhere in the world. The main theme of the characters of these fables is the inclusion of different and several stories within the same framework of a single story, like Chinese boxes. The characters of the main story relate the various tales to justify their own special views and opinions of conduct, morals and ethics.

The entire book of the *Panchatantra* contains humour that transfers all sorts of human action to the animal kingdom. One story contains about the character of half-men and half-animals devoting themselves to the study of the Vedas, practices and rules of rituals and ceremonies. They exchange views about gods, sages and rituals between themselves. During the discussion suddenly their violent animal nature breaks out and they begin to fight. The moral of the story suggests that men are part of animal nature that can flare up with slight provocation and should be kept in check by contemplation and meditation. It can easily destroy or disrupt the fabric of the society.

There is another story of the *Panchatantra* that relates a dispute between a sparrow and a monkey. A pious cat was invited as a referee to settle the dispute between them. Such fables inspire confidence and importance of virtue in life. There is another story of a musical donkey bragging about his dancing and musical talents. Nobody took any notice of his talents as they were busy with their own work and routine and had no time to appreciate his talents. This disappointed the donkey and he committed suicide. The moral of the story is that one should not boast about one's success in front of others.

Another story relates about a group of monkeys shivering in the cold winter of the forest, with rain and clouds hovering over their heads. They did not find a place for shelter. Some of the monkeys began to collect some dry berries (small, dry, shining fruit) looking like sparks of fire. A bird was watching the useless efforts of the monkeys and shouted, "You fools, there are no sparks of fire in the berries. They are only dry fruits and you will not protect yourself from these clouds in this manner. It is better to look for some cave or spot in the forest." Hearing this an old monkey said, "It is not your business." The bird replied, "It is an useless efforts of yours." One of the monkeys got angry over the repeated interference and seized the bird and smashed it with the stone. The bird died. Many other such stories are also found in *Hitopadesha*, borrowed from the *Panchatantra*. There is a very interesting story of an ass and a tiger. Similar stories are found in large quantities in Buddhist literature in which animals play a very important role to educate and enlighten the people.

It is now better to look at some of the stories of the distinguished French author, La Fontaine, who has adopted from the *Panchatantra* and changed the characters but kept the story line intact. A well-known story is of a milkmaid who was carrying the milkpot on her head to sell in the market, and building castles in the air, of experiencing joy with the proceeds of the sale—to buy a house, educate her children in a famous school and live like a rich person. In a moment of joy she stumbled and dropped her milkpot from her head. In the *Panchatantra* the same story has been described about a brahmin who collected rice by begging and kept the rice in a bowl. He dreamt that he would sell it during famine and earn a lot of money, buy a house, cattle and live like a famous man. In a moment of joy he dropped the bowl and all the rice scattered on the ground. Another story of La Fontaine has also been taken from the *Panchatantra*. It is of a jackal who found dead bodies of a bear and a hunter besides the bow of the hunter. He decided to take the bow first. As he was trying to separate the bowstring from the hunter, it pierced his head and died instantly. La Fontaine used a wolf instead of the jackal of the *Panchatantra* in his book.

Every story of the *Panchatantra* carries a message that could be used and helpful to educate the conduct of human behaviour. They may not be religious, ethical or intellectual, but certainly possess the message of right conduct, transforming human behaviour.

The fables of ancient Sanskrit literature are the most important weapons of political and social instruction. It is only Europe that has exploited and mastered the technique and the wisdom of Indian fables. They are most successful because their subject matter is based on laughter and amusement. Their beauty and strength lie on the understanding of an ordinary human being.

Epilogue

Once four men were queuing up at the door of heaven. When the receptionist opened the door and saw four men waiting to enter into heaven, he asked the first man, "What have you done to go into heaven?" The man replied, "I believe in God. I read holy books and observe all the religious activities such as pray and fast. I have neither committed crime in thoughts nor in action. At times I punish myself to concentrate in meditation and prayer. People respect and accept me as a representative of God." "You cannot enter into heaven as you are selfish. Believing in God and observing religious activities are not sufficient to live in heaven. Go back to earth and suffer earthly pains," the receptionist answered.

"What have you done to enter into heaven?" the receptionist asked the second man.

"I believe in God, the only God, and recite my holy book and pray five times a day. I command believers to submit to the Will of God. I engage in battles to spread the religion of my prophet. My religion is the only religion, which guarantees a place in the heaven for believers who fight for God as martyrs. I punish non-believers, idol-worshippers, pass death sentence to those who insult my religion and prophet. The believers who die in the ways of God I glorify them as martyrs."

"There is no place for you in heaven as you use authority to terrorise people in the name of God. You judge and divide people into believers and non-believers. God does not preach division, rather He bestows wisdom and knowledge towards unity with Him and does not interfere in the affairs of the human society or in the natural process. You take away their freedom and make them slaves and dependent on your group authority," the receptionist replied.

"What have you done to enter into heaven?" the receptionist asked the third man. "I am the head of the hierarchy of my religious order and express opinions and statements, which are carried out by the followers of my faith. I have fully developed religious orders that function in strict discipline. It helps the poor and the needy and provides food, shelter and medical care, irrespective of colour, creed and religions. Our activists are dedicated missionaries who have renounced the pleasures and luxuries of society to bring sinners into the virtuous path. Our prophet took all the sins of the society upon himself to redeem the sins of the people so that they can enter into the kingdom of God. We ask people to confess their sins and lead a virtuous life on earth."

"You cannot go into heaven. You exploit the weakness of man so that they may join your crowd under the heavy burden of obligation. God is inside man and not outside somewhere in the charity or prayer. They are aids only for the welfare of society and not the realisation of God inside. God does not exist only in a large cathedral, mosque or temple. God is realised in every piece of brick, which built the holy places. God's existence can be felt in every particle of sand or atom and in every wave that rises in the ocean," the receptionist answered.

"What have you done to enter into heaven?" the receptionist turned to the last man. "I am neither a man of letters nor of substance in the eyes of the society. I do not read holy books regularly or pray in a temple, mosque or church. I realise the presence of God in every object of nature, animals and human society. I cannot say that there is a God in the stone of the temple or in the empty space of the mosque and in the cross of the church. These are only names and forms for me. One cannot describe God in words or forms as words or forms are limited in meaning. But they all share the same, as God exists in all of them. There is a unity in all of them. When I stand at the beach and see the rising waves in the sea I feel a sensation for the existence of God in them. When I stand in the garden and appreciate the beauty and smell flowers, they provide me divinely pleasure. Every human being, whether he is a sinner or saint, has the same spark of big fire, i.e., God is within me. I am God." The receptionist said, "You can go and live in heaven." We always reserve a place for such people who realise God in everything, as everything is the manifestation of God.

(2)

There was a king who had a multi-religious population in his kingdom. He was very worried as the religious groups used to fight among themselves. The Hindus were killing Muslims, the Protestants were killing Catholics, the Muslims were killing Jews, the Sunnis were killing Shi'ites and vice versa. The king had tried various measures to stop the killing of the groups but it was of no use. At last he had decided to call a conference of respectable people of his country as well as religious leaders to find out solutions. The conference discussed the violence and murders in the name of religion to find a respectable solution and failed miserably to reach any suitable remedy for the destruction and massacre of the various religious groups. At the end of the conference, the king addressed them and demanded answers to his three questions, from the chief priest of the kingdom.

1. What was before God?
2. Where does He live?

3. What does God do?

"Bring me the answers within seven days. If your answers convince the delegates of the conference you will be rewarded generously, and if your answers fail to convince them you will be hanged before the conference."

The delegates were astonished to hear such fundamental and complex questions about God. The conference was dismissed with the request to reassemble a week later at the same time in the same hall to listen to the answers. The head priest went home with a heavy heart and in great distress. When he reached home his wife did not recognise her husband as he was looking 20 years older than his age. His face was visibly shaken. She enquired the reason for his condition. The head priest narrated the proceedings of the conference along with the questions.

He failed to find the right answers, that could even satisfy him, as God is invisible and unseen. Therefore he decided that it was better to commit suicide rather than to be hanged before the conference of the wise men. On the seventh day he left home to commit suicide. When he was ready to jump into the river someone shouted from behind, "Stop. It is sin to kill or to commit suicide. Moreover, it is the greatest sin when killing or suicide is carried out in the name of religion or God." When the priest looked behind, he saw a shepherd boy of 13 or 14 years old. The priest explained to the boy the reason of his suicide. The boy replied that these questions were very simple and he was ready to give the correct answers to the entire satisfaction of the king and the delegates of the conference. At first the priest did not take the boy seriously for he felt that an unlearned shepherd boy cannot answer such complicated questions to satisfy the learned men. After some persuasion the priest accepted the child's offer and went with him to the conference, which was waiting for him. The king asked the priest, "Did you discover the answers to my questions?" "Sire, I feel ashamed to give the answers of such simple questions. The boy who has come with me is willing to give the answer to your questions." The boy was asked to stand in the middle of the hall to give the answers to the questions.

The boy requested the king, "Sire, there is a condition before I answer your questions. Whatever I ask you during the question it should be carried out." The king gave his consent to the boy.

"What is your first question?" the boy asked the king.

"What was before God?"

"Count the numbers from one to five."

"One, two, three, four and five."

"Stop."

"What is before five?"

"Four."

"What is before four?"

"Three."

"What is before three?"

"Two."

"What is before two?"

"One."

"What is before one?"

"Nothing. Zero"

"This is the answer of your first question—that there is nothing before God as there is nothing before zero. What is your second question?" the boy asked the king.

"Where does He (God) live?"

"Would you please provide me a glass of milk?"

The milk was brought to the boy.

"Does butter exist in this milk?"

"Yes."

"Can you see the butter in the milk?"

"No."

"Can you take out the butter from the milk?"

"Yes, but certain acts should be followed before extracting the butter from the milk."

"This is the answer to your second question—that God exists everywhere like butter in the milk and one has to follow certain acts to find God. What is your third question?"

"What does God do?"

"Would you please come down from the throne and take off all your clothes and crown?" the boy asked the king. The boy had taken off all his clothes and gave them to the king to wear. The boy put on the clothes of the king and occupied the throne and declared himself the king. Now he issued an order that this man should be arrested and kept him in prison to be hanged the next morning. As he was being taken away by the chief of the police, the boy asked him to stop.

"This is the answer to your third question—that the king becomes the criminal and a shepherd boy becomes the king."

The king was very pleased with the answers and asked the assembly to express the opinion in favour or against the answers. There was not a single vote against the answers.

Next day the king issued a decree, "God lives in every heart as well as in every atom of the universe like the butter in the milk. If anyone exploits and fights in the name of religion he will be hanged and his property will be confiscated. Religion is a personal matter and it should remain a personal matter. It has nothing to do with the social or political matters of the society." Within six months his kingdom became very peaceful and began to make good progress.